'Ben Tallon
story to life *in vivid ...*

The endless brush-offs, the terminal lack of cash,
the excruciating and crushing cold calls, the impassable
brick wall between you and the elusive business you want
to break into, and the surreal and random nature of working
in media and the folks who live in that world. Ben brilliantly
encapsulates all of this and more in a series of perfectly
worded snapshots illustrating his journey from eager young
graduate to successful creative professional.

Aside from his obvious talents as a creative, it's obvious
when reading that he had to call into play all of his natural
tenacity and sense of humour (both of which Ben has in spades)
just to stay on board the emotional roller coaster where
others would have come flying off.

A funny and informative guidebook for anyone who's
thinking of trying to break into the creative industries,
and a highly evocative reminder for anyone who's
forgotten what it felt like to go though.'
MARK RADER, CHANNEL 4/MTV

'Very insightful and entertaining. Some great anecdotes.
You paint an excellent picture of being a creative in
the real world once you have graduated.'
HAYDEN RUSSELL, ART DIRECTOR, MIXMAG

'The author's spontaneity, mayhem wit and enthusiasm shine
through the manuscript - but its core is one of very useful
lessons for making it as a creative freelancer.

It's a great choice of subject and the way he treats it
from an intensely personal point of view - beginning with

the misery of the lost art school graduate flailing about in the real world - makes an enjoyable read.

I've heard, and my students have been enraptured by so many of these stories over the past few years - maybe I shouldn't confess this, but when Ben's not in attendance, I often find myself repeating them to my illustration students. I know the rest of what he has to say will be wild, crazy... and eminently good advice!'

BILL WRIGHT, COURSE LEADER, ENHANCED ILLUSTRATION, CENTRAL SAINT MARTINS COLLEGE

'Funny, gripping and memorable, this book quickly draws you into the highs, lows and madness of creative freelancing. Perfect for those who have been on a similar journey or those who are starting out in their career, this book mixes real life advice with humorous anecdotes. I couldn't put it down'

SARAH BRADLEY, CO-FOUNDER, THE ART OF NEW BUSINESS

'This book really is a fascinating insight into a creative journey. It is full of random funny quips and tales and it's inspiring to see someone in the industry taking an unconventional path, which makes for a more interesting read, I could relate to. It's proof that if someone takes the less conventional path, it doesn't mean they won't be successful, or even more so. I think society instills a fear in you, that if you differ from the norm, you are either a huge success and make it as a one off example, or you are a failure.

Being honest, I totally get the whole rock star status of great illustrators; some of these are more impressive and idolized than movie stars. I probably aspire to these levels much more than movie stars or celebrities. Ben is awesome and really boosted my morale and it is amazing to read that he has been through the same ringer and had similar experiences; this book made me feel reassured that I am on the right path!

It really is a fascinating and captivating read. I would love to see the illustrations and images the author references; the early works, the life drawings and so on, just to see and understand how Ben has developed.

He really has a lovely informal writing style that is brutally honest and relevant to the reader, which I think is really important for the subject of this story.'

ASHLEY DODD, STUDENT,
UNIVERSITY OF HERTFORDSHIRE

'I am a big fan of Ben's work, so for me to read about his journey and the stories behind the pieces of work that have served as a source of inspiration for me over the past few years, was really interesting.

And as a recent graduate myself, I can relate to how Ben felt when he graduated and they way he describes his thoughts and feelings during this time made me laugh.

I found it helpful when he reflected on the stuff that he learned after each chapter as well. Overall I think it's really inspirational and I think it's written really well.'

RHYS LOWRY, GRADUATE,
ATRIUM: CARDIFF SCHOOL OF CREATIVE
AND CULTURAL INDUSTRIES

'So easy and enjoyable to read. Ben is very likeable and you want him to do well, an underdog of sorts. It keeps you hooked. Also, he's pretty funny.

Champagne and Wax Crayons *has given me more reassurance and fired up my desire to go for it - as of this afternoon I now have a portfolio with the Association Of Illustrators!'*

KATIE DONALD, ILLUSTRATOR,
WHAT KATIE DREW

CHAMPAGNE AND WAX CRAYONS

RIDING THE MADNESS OF THE CREATIVE INDUSTRIES

Published by
LID Publishing Limited
The Record Hall, Studio 204,
16-16a Baldwins Gardens,
London EC1N 7RJ, UK

info@lidpublishing.com
www.lidpublishing.com

A member of:

www.businesspublishersroundtable.com

Reprinted in 2018, 2019

Printed in Great Britain by TJ International
ISBN: 978-1-907794-93-3

Cover design: Ben Tallon
Page design: Laura Hawkins

CHAMPAGNE AND WAX CRAYONS

RIDING THE MADNESS OF THE CREATIVE INDUSTRIES

BEN TALLON

MADRID | MEXICO CITY | LONDON
NEW YORK | BUENOS AIRES
BOGOTA | SHANGHAI | NEW DELHI

For my family,
who allowed me the freedom
to play and make mistakes

free·lance

n. also **freelance**

1. *A person who sells services to employers without a long-term commitment to any of them.*

2. *An uncommitted independent, as in politics or social life.*

3. *A medieval mercenary.*

v. **free·lanced, free·lanc·ing, free·lanc·es**

CONTENTS

ACKNOWLEDGEMENTS

If I listed all the people that made writing a book possible, the thing would be released in two parts.

Thanks to LID Publishing, David Woods, Martin Liu, Laura Hawkins and Sarah Wild for the belief and hard work.

I'd be nothing without all the mad-heads who've believed in and influenced me along the way, who've made the ride so fun, rewarding and bearable in the bleak spells. You all know who you are.

A heartfelt thank you to the kind people who took the time to contribute to this book: Dave Hilton, Dirty Freud, Danny Allison, Sam Price, Ken Garland, Victoria Pearce, Roger Browning, Mark Rader, Sarah Bradley, Bill Wright, Katie Donald, Rhys Lowry, Ashley Dodd, Hayden Russell, Kevin Bannon and Andy Cotterill.

Thanks again to my family. Their encouragement, patience, lack of pressure to do anything that I didn't love, and their sacrifices, were integral in enabling me to live my dream. Their selfless support for myself and my brother, who suffered an upbringing with a bitter Leeds fan and still sent me wrestling video-tapes to university each week, was special.

FOREWORD

BY DAVID HILTON, VP CREATIVE DIRECTOR
OF DIGITAL MEDIA AT WORLD WRESTLING
ENTERTAINMENT. FORMER CREATIVE DIRECTOR
OF *MAXIM* AND *STUFF* MAGAZINES.

The only time I ever really knew what I wanted to do with my life was at seven years old when I was determined to be a WWII German soldier because the uniforms were cooler than those worn by their plastic British counterparts. Since then, and to this day, I have never had a plan for what's next.

My school careers adviser had suggested that because I was good at art, becoming a painter and decorator would probably be my best path. I find that almost as amusing now, as did my dad, who was sat next to me in the meeting at the time. Instead, he drove me around a handful of printers and small graphic design outfits in and around the Bolton area and I was lucky enough to secure a Youth Training Scheme with one of them. Being honest though, I had no idea what graphic design was.

Growing up, my greatest love was music, and thanks to my cousin Mark, and much to the horror of my parents, I was steered into the punk scene, which was rich with incredibly thoughtful visuals and amazing sleeve designs. Later, my obsession with design really flourished with the discovery of the 4AD record label. Vaughan Oliver, my favourite designer and biggest influence to this day, opened my eyes not only to an entirely new way of thinking about my creative work but also to a whole genre of bands like The Pixies, Cocteau Twins, This Mortal Coil and so on, that I wouldn't have heard otherwise.

As it was impossible to apply this kind of design to the projects I was handed at work, I searched for another outlet to allow my own style to develop – by combining my interests, music and design, I started my own music fanzine.

It only dawned on me in recent years that this project was what spawned a 25-year career in the publishing industry - writing up band interviews, shooting and editing photos, and hours painstakingly kerning headlines using WH Smith's rub-down lettering sheets for my layouts.

Lucky breaks are, of course, great career enhancers if you're fortunate enough to have them and mine came in the shape of London based company Letraset™, type designers and manufacturers of graphic design products, purchasing the company I was working for at the time. That move took me to London but was short-lived, ironically, due to the rise of Apple and its introduction of desktop publishing completely revolutionizing the industry. Little did I know at the time that was while Apple was busy putting me out of work I would soon become dependent on it for life. I had only been in the capital for eight months, working in Sweden for three of them, when Letraset™ started to feel the pinch and had to make staff cuts, including me. My mind had already been blown by the people I had met in London and I wasn't ready to head back north just yet.

The day after I lost my job, I posted (exactly 200) speculative letters to any and every design studio, publisher and who-the-hell-knows what else, in hope that I could secure any position to help subsidize my exorbitant Finsbury Park rent.

An early Sunday morning call from Dennis Publishing proved to be my saviour and I spent the next 18 years in the whirlwind employment of the most inspiring man for whom I will ever work. Felix Dennis, maverick publisher and poet, who built an empire worth hundreds of millions of pounds.

'Do it first, apologize later - I don't care if you fail, all I care is you try' is surely the only time I will receive a brief that genuinely terrified and yet enabled me to realize my potential as a designer. He had an incredible knack of dictating exactly what he wanted but still giving enough creative freedom to allow you to completely own every project. To my knowledge, I only failed him once, and boy did he let me know about it.

Little did I realize, I had just landed a role that would give me the best education imaginable for a designer of my age. I spent the next eight years working in the marketing department for more than 25 publications, encompassing a huge variety of subject matter including technology, sport, politics, humour, gaming, fitness, automotive and so on.

Learning to adapt quickly and design with very different disciplines was my steepest, and most valuable, learning curve to date. Jimmy Egerton, my design director at the time, hammered into me the importance of designing appropriately for the reader/user, and as long as I always kept that in mind, I could then apply my own aesthetic and design myself silly.

At the time, the lads magazine culture hit the UK with the launch of *Loaded*, *FHM* and *Maxim*. Young men had begun to buy magazines by the hundreds of thousands every month and a whole new career path opened up to me... *Maxim US*.

Through hard work, fulfilling briefs and having gained the trust of the board at Dennis Publishing, I was presented with the opportunity of moving to the US to be part of a team to launch *Maxim* magazine in America. It was obviously, a proposition I couldn't resist. The men's magazine revolution hadn't happened stateside and Felix Dennis was in a hurry to launch first. With *Maxim* selling more than two million copies per month, he later, very humbly, credited its meteoric rise with 'I was just the first guy into the desert with a beer truck'.

It was a baptism of fire. Outside my role as a marketing designer, I had previously only worked on one issue of one magazine before being entrusted with *Maxim*'s launch in the US.

I had to think on my feet and live and breathe the job. Luckily, I barely knew a soul in New York and was able to completely submerge myself, without distraction, into the greatest education I have ever received.

Two weeks in every month I was frantically designing magazines, day and night, while assembling a small team of designers and photo editors. The other two weeks spent art directing celebrity photo shoots in Los Angeles while discovering how the world of publicists and agents worked.

I very quickly realized that hiring strong talent was the only way I was going to keep my head above water. Bringing experienced magazine designers over from the UK was an instant hit - we presented a different design sensibility and were able to deliver *Maxim* in a way that prevented it from resembling any of the US men's titles.

We were also handed a very healthy budget and were fortunate enough to work with some of the best photographers in the business. We were commissioning and directing celebrity shoots with Antoine Verglas, Dominick Guillemot, Santé D'Orazio, Nigel Parry, Patrick Hoelck, Robert Maxwell and James White to name a few. It was a golden period I will never forget or take for granted – these guys made it easy. All of a sudden, we had a magazine that swaggered like the upstart it was intended to be.

We worked hard and played even harder. Knowing that the industry's eyes were on us and that we had the best jobs in the world, enabled us to take advantage of, but also carefully navigate, the fact that bars are open until 4am in New York City. If I'm ever in the position to assemble such a talented and funny team of people again I will be very lucky.

I'm not a great believer in the popular perception that 'it's not what you know, it's who you know'. I think the 'what you know' absolutely has to be gathered first and the 'who you know' will follow in time. Hard work, talent, and a love of what you do will bring the contacts and relationships you need to maintain throughout your entire career.

One way or another, I stay in touch with a huge number of mentors, employees and associates with whom I have collaborated with over the years. Be it a quick message via social media, taking time to shoot out a quick email to congratulate people on their promotions, meeting up at design events or getting together for a quick pint after work.

Football has also been an amazing networking tool for me over the years. After my move from Bolton to London, for example, I met many new friends through playing for a variety of media related leagues but also because people delighted in making fun of the Bolton Wanderers fan.

I completely lost that outlet after my move to New York due to their zero tolerance policy for 'soccer' (at the time) and my distaste for American sport(s) which made me realize just how important it is to make connections through any common interests possible.

And that's how I met Ben Tallon. As creative director of World Wrestling Entertainment (WWE), I receive dozens of emails from photographers and illustrators, many of which are obsessive fans, but Ben was probably the most persistent of all, which ultimately paid off. I loved his style but had to wait for the right project to come up before being able to commission him. When the opportunity arose I took another look at his website... First, I noticed in his bio that his dream job was 'to illustrate a WrestleMania poster'... second, that he was UK based. That was enough of a connection for me to call him and want to give him the job. We also had a geographical connection in that we are both from the North and have been long suffering fans of our respective teams.

As a lifelong WWE fan, Ben loves the brand, always delivers amazing work to deadline and regularly pitches great ideas, which generates more commissions for him. For example, the time I needed hand-painted typography in a particular style, Ben worked at mastering the style to secure that job and has since added it to his repertoire and is now regularly commissioned for that style alone. He has an incredible knack of staying true to his own creative aesthetic but also has the talent and flexibility to merge his style with current trends.

That's what it is all about. The most enjoyable part of my career to date has been working with the people with whom I have been lucky enough to collaborate; especially the young designers, illustrators and photographers I have been able to give opportunities to. There is nothing more satisfying that seeing a young designer's face when you say 'congratulations, you've got the job', or handing someone a magazine containing their first published work.

I think it is equally important to give back to people starting out, as it is to draw experience from peers along the way. I'll never forget the people who have helped get me along but also fully appreciate that it is my responsibility to pass on opportunities to others. For me, that's genuinely the most satisfying part of all.

INTRODUCTION

People always look slightly befuddled when I tell them I'm a freelance illustrator, in that 'oh that's cool' (but what does that actually mean) kind of way. I don't really know either, to tell you the truth. The 31-year-old child in me wants to tell them I'm an art mercenary. I've yet to find the guts required to actually do it. So instead, I explain that 'people pay me to create artwork for visual media and I can do that from anywhere in the world, provided I have an internet connection'.

Seven years ago, I wrapped up my education at the University of Central Lancashire and squared up to real life for the first time, without my student loan as a shield.

Callously kicked out of my single bed and into the real world, I found myself shivering and clutching my red-ribboned scroll, wearing the silly mortar board, with only scraps of my bank overdraft left over. Now that I had my sparkling 2:1 degree in illustration, countless beautiful women, cash-rich employers and shoals of paparazzi would surely follow any moment now? But they didn't.

That was the vision, but in the material world, the rain just kept on peppering my single-glaze, end-of-terrace bedroom window as I stared at another cool designer's website on my computer screen, struggling to find any form of motivation. No career revelations. It wasn't that I didn't know *what* I wanted to do – it was more a complete lack of knowing where to begin in my quest to make a living from anything the last seven years had taught me.

As an aspiring illustrator, a profession with perilously few positions of employment, I didn't even have a job market to look at, just a really weak portfolio and £15,000 of student debt. The sensory overload you get when you look at the thousands of stylish artists with better portfolios and cooler haircuts than yours is overwhelming and frightening. Sitting in the dark in your underpants looking at their achievements wouldn't drain your confidence with each click if you could just see the journey that led to them to the finished product. After all, even the masters must have started *somewhere,* right?

It took a few years to become savvy enough, but eventually it dawned on me that there was a certain amount of clever editing at play here. I wasn't the only person who gradually learned how to hide all the difficult bits in freelancing and show the passer by only a heavyweight client list or a cool press photograph to make it look as if I was definitely not panicking under the weight of financial pressure. It's not bullshit, it's more smoke and mirrors, similar to how 'celebrity magazines' routinely convince millions of people that a celebrity is having an alcohol-fuelled breakdown by publishing only the still frame of the perfect moment they blinked as they crossed their legs in the back of the taxi.

Back in 2006, nobody could have convinced me I'd live out several childhood dreams within five years and now, when I teach, I see the same fear in the eyes of any student who gives a shit about doing something with their creative degree.

Theoretically preparing anyone for the schizophrenic nature of creative freelancing in the 21st century is wasted energy - how can you teach someone certainties about a world governed by opinions, trends and whims? I tried the 'how-to' textbooks and they gave me a decent overview about identifying clients, refining my brand and marketing my work, but their ability to impart advice abruptly ends when you're looking for a way past the demoralizing feeling that comes when nobody has replied to the first 60 emails you've just been told how to send.

What time would teach me is that the only way to learn your place in the arts is by getting out and *doing it*. Trouble is, that's all well and good if you know what *it* is! Most people do not and it takes lots of trial, error and unplanned f**k ups to find your place - every single person deals with the madness of the creative industries in their own deeply personal way.

These days, I'm lucky enough to receive kind emails from people who like my work. Many ask the same questions about my inspirations, self-promotion and finding work as a freelancer. So, instead of trying to tell you how to do *anything*, I've decided to write down my last seven years, because revealing one of the stories behind the portfolios might just be the best way to help someone who is a feeling slightly daunted by it all.

Trying to earn a living from your passion is one of the greatest challenges of all and, in the words of DJ and filmmaker, Don Letts, when your play becomes your work you've reached the peak of civilization.

DANNY ALLISON: PHOTOGRAPHER AND ILLUSTRATOR, *TIME* MAGAZINE, BUDWEISER, BBC, EMI RECORDS

'I failed my GCSE in art. I was too busy skateboarding, that was my art back then. I would express myself through my boarding. Call it a sport, you can call it an art or whatever, nobody really knows... I picked that up at the age of about 15. You know what? I didn't realize it back then, but the group of skateboarders I hung around with were the weird group in society. They'd all been sort of excluded from everything else - football matches and all of that, they just kind of congregated in one place.

I didn't see it that way at the time, but it was a creative hub that was preparing me way before I considered anything outside of skating as a career. You'd be around creative writing, creative talking, graffiti, art. It's crazy, you just think, 'everyone is like this.' As you get older, it makes you go, 'no, nobody was like that at all.' All these unique groups of skateboarders in the world, they have that same bond in creativity.'

CHAPTER 1. WAX CRAYONS

There wasn't a great deal to do growing up where I did, in Keighley, a small West Yorkshire town, where some people still shout abuse at you for wearing any hat other than a baseball cap. If the sun was out, I was running around outside playing football; when it rained, I'd be inside sketching with my brother. That's about it. I grew up with a creative mother and a football-mad father in the 1980s. It set the tone early doors and these two pillars of my personal and professional life have just kind of stayed with me. As a 31-year-old man, I still remember dates by anchoring them to a WWE pay-per-view event or Leeds United fixtures.

My uncles and dad were pretty handy at drawing and my grandparents really encouraged me once they noticed my creative side. As a kid, it seems somehow cooler when adults draw or paint with you. My uncle Ray and I would have drawing competitions with a pre-agreed theme and he was much better than me, but his weekly endorsements of my steady improvement fired me up so much to try be as good as he was that I would feverishly practise until late at night, developing faster. The downside to this conviction was that I used to flip the board during family games at the exact moment I knew a game was lost, forcing my parents to give me my marching orders, the earliest sign of a fierce competitive streak. Teachers will try to stamp that out, but the good ones will simply channel it better.

I've been obsessed with professional wrestling and football from an early age but I've only ever been average at the latter. One Sunday, when we were 16, two friends and I made a speculative three-leg journey to Sheffield to take part in a pro-wrestling class we had seen advertised in a UK wrestling magazine. As skinny teenagers, we were tantalized by how glamorous and easy it looks on the telly. In a freezing cold, smelly Sheffield gym, it was different. The place had that vintage sweat smell you get in affordable gyms, decades of fossilized graft embedded into its very foundations. We had no heavy metal theme music and nobody provided extra drama with colour commentary. I got to do Bret 'Hitman' Hart's flying clothesline though, which was cool. My friend from down the road was power-bombed on a crash mat and strained his neck a bit. He moaned the whole way home, so we didn't bother going again.

After my last roll of the dice, the idea of a career in sport was quickly abandoned, so all that was left for me was art. By that point, I had already completed three-quarters of my physical education GCSE, so I thought I'd better hang around and sign up for the following year's art GCSE while everyone else stayed on schedule. I needed the qualification to get into art college, so I did it alongside a half-arsed attempt at an intermediate business course to fill the time, which I never completed. I hated the school art teaching methods and didn't get along with the tutor, with whom I'd had numerous run-ins during art classes in previous years. I struggled through with the required C grade and couldn't wait to leave.

It was at school that I had my first glimpse of how my artwork might actually have a place in the wider world. My playfully antagonistic side surfaced in drawing and regularly landed me in trouble. Teachers don't appreciate being sketched in a rabbit hutch, with their head on a rodent body, but the reaction of uproar it drew from fellow students was too addictive to ignore, so I did it anyway. This one teacher, we nicknamed 'Weasel.' I drew him accordingly and one of the other kids snatched the piece from me, depositing it through his classroom window. For two weeks, I saw it sat there, on the window ledge, hidden only by the classroom blinds. Every time, it sent a rush of fear through me, the kind that makes you weak at the knees. One day it disappeared and we were all summoned to Weasel's classroom at lunchtime. It didn't take long for him to establish that it was my handiwork and he sent us away having concluded his investigation. For two weeks, I was jelly-legged at the prospect of suspension from school, which wouldn't have been unwarranted given the harshness of the drawing.

One day, a messenger arrives in my form class and asks if I can go and see Weasel. He stares me down, watching me tremble before telling me that I have real talent and that the drawing made him laugh a lot. My 'punishment' was to create him a unique poster to advertise an upcoming school talk on dyslexia. To this day, I respect the hell out of that guy and he cleverly made me take the first step in the right direction in creating more purposeful work in years to come.

Parental pressure to take a more traditional academic path was alien to me, unlike for some of the other kids who were really good at art or sport, but had been pushed towards safer, 'proper' subjects. I felt sorry for them. I was only encouraged to do anything academic when I showed a natural interest in it. My parents said that if it made me happy, then I should give it my all and that would be enough for them. I suppose I took it for granted at that point, but if they'd thrown the 'real job' mantra at me, I shudder to think what I'd be doing with my time today. My only passions were sport and art and it takes real trust for parents to allow a kid to follow a dream.

A creative person's resolve is often fragile, especially early on. In those days, there are only vulnerable exteriors, easily pierced by words and opinions. In my young, naïve position, I lacked any kind of career direction, underachieving in my GCSE exams thanks to spending more than 100 hours playing *Final Fantasy 7* on the Sony Playstation. But with hindsight, it was the total lack of pressure and my love of that video game, that allowed me the freedom to stumble my way through school and into Keighley College and sign up for a *BTEC National Diploma in Graphic Design* after tutors saw my game character drawings during a work experience placement at the college in 1999.

- Freedom to follow the heart is crucial when finding your creative path.

- If you enjoy being creative, do not be dissuaded by school art, no matter how shit it may seem. College and university are very different and give you more creative freedom.

- You may have to defy your parents if they've never encountered the arts in their own lives. Their questioning is well meant, but art is an unknown - the scariest thing of all to most people.

- Learn from, and spend time with, people who share your creative interests. Other viewpoints can teach you lots of valuable things, do not shy away from honest feedback from both more and less experienced people.

- If you're competitive, it is a positive career trait, so channel it well.

- Pursue the things that you naturally enjoy doing or take an interest in; do not overlook the simple things you do for pleasure, in your free time. Film, TV, games and sport are as valid as maths, English and science. Passion is the ultimate motivator.

- Wrestling classes in Sheffield are not as glamorous as wrestling looks on the telly.

VICTORIA PEARCE: FORMER FASHION AND PHOTOGRAPHY AGENT, CURRENT AGENT AT ILLUSTRATION LTD

'The original reason I wanted to go into fashion design was because I loved magazines. It was the age of The Face, I-D, Blitz when I was growing up in a little village in the Cotswolds. Pre-internet and Facebook, that was my lifeline. You'd go to the local newsagent and buy the latest magazine and see these people hanging out and what they were all wearing. Through these pages, you could see that there were these other style tribes out there that you could immediately identify with. I was really into the rockabilly rock 'n' roll scene.

Now, just about everyone knows what a stylist is, but back then I don't know if that term had even been given a definition. I think I wanted to be a stylist, only I didn't know what a stylist was. I wanted to be involved in the making of these images I loved in the magazines and I thought that studying fashion was the route to that.'

CHAPTER 2. NAKED BECKHAM

I was 14 when I first tried to make any money from my art. My childhood friends were from the adjacent streets. We lived next to a woollen mill and the houses we lived in were the mill worker's houses, old Yorkshire stone terraces. One mate and I spent a lot of time at the mill when the workers had gone home.

Methods of making a quick few quid outside of my paper round and the occasional glass-collecting shift at my friend's sister's boozer were scarce and we couldn't afford to go and watch Leeds United on less than £10 per week. We hung out with two sisters and their cousins, who were always annoying us by swooning over the likes of David Beckham and assorted boy band members.

One night, sitting on the roof of the bin sheds at the bottom of the streets, my friend pitched a seemingly golden business idea. He felt that there was money to be made if I could add a twist to the pencil portraits I was always drawing in my spare time. He said that instead of drawing Leeds players, I should depict Beckham completely naked. He was sure the girls would part with pocket money to own such a deviant masterpiece and the idea seemed infallible for a couple of nights. My friend's role in the deal was that he would run the sales and marketing side of the business. If Beckham was a success, we could roll out the idea further. In a way, he was my first agent. I borrowed one of my brother's Manchester United poster magazines for reference and covertly drew one A3-sized naked Beckham with an outrageously enhanced member. It took me four days to complete. I hid it in the *Shoot 1995 Annual,* knowing that many difficult questions would be directed at me if my parents found it. On the fifth day, I panicked and shredded it before even my friend had seen it and decided that a part-time job at Netto supermarket on top of my paper round may be a better option for the time being.

ART COLLEGE

At 17 years old, I hadn't properly considered the possibility that my love of art could ever blossom into a career, save for the dyslexia poster incident. You just don't understand how artists, designers and the world of visual communication operate when you're that young. I went to college because that was the next thing most people were doing and art was the only subject of interest to me after the school bell rang.

Keighley is a mill town where the vast majority of work is either in retail or trades such as plumbing, joinery and construction. You had to be streetwise – in a small town where people are not afraid to say what they think, it can be easy to feel a bit intimidated if you're reserved. Fights outside pubs were not uncommon sights most weekends. The ability to talk to people you don't necessarily know serves you well in business and that would eventually become a very valuable skill for me. College was my first experience of spending time in a place where you could be yourself openly without worrying about what someone might think or say.

Spending the majority of my week with people of different ages and varying personalities, all with a common interest in creativity, was refreshing. Seemingly overnight, I was the original free-range man. We were allowed to take a break whenever we wanted. You can't claim to be an adult with any credibility until you hold a styrofoam cup of tea or coffee, standing around in corridors or smoking areas.

College was full of people wearing a variety of clothes, listening to bands I hadn't heard of. The BTEC was labelled graphic design but it covered a wide range of artistic disciplines where the staff encouraged you to get stuck into a load of different mediums and explore them all, such as 2D design, web design, sculpture, film, printing techniques and unconventional mediums. They threw in a photography course for free but I saw that as an opportunity to go to the pub during the day and get smashed with my mate who was studying bricklaying in the warehouse opposite my corner of the college.

I sometimes reflect on not taking that photography course very seriously, but in my defence, there was something to be said about those college outings to the pub. I'd gone from dressing down for fear of attracting unwanted comments, to having these liberating, boozy conversations about music and badly researched politics after two beers, in the corner of the pub with new friends, wearing whatever I wanted and calling myself an artist. Yes, I missed out on photography skills, but I was growing as a person. I embraced all of it.

It felt perfect. Suddenly everything went unchecked and despite the unwelcome invasion of hangovers in my life, I was all but banned from drawing bowls of fruit, in the name of originality. That was a fair enough trade to me.

Bill Parker ran the BTEC and was the first adult, aside from those in my family, to notice my love of drawing. I was about to learn a big lesson from him; that if a person likes you or sees passion and a desire to learn, they are more inclined to meet you halfway.

Every time I took any steps forward by loosening up my creative style, I'd have a dramatic relapse and turn up to the project critique session with a drawing so stiff it looked like I'd made it with scaffolding. I just couldn't shake the common misconception that 'laborious and complex' equates to good quality. I was aspiring to hyper-realism and expert detail in everything I did. One midweek afternoon, my tutors really attacked me. Nigel, one of the support tutors, approached me after the critique session was done and asked for a word in the next door room. Still only a year out of school, I shuffled in with my tail between my legs, anticipating a harsh word for going missing and getting drunk each Thursday, or some other misdemeanor.

Nigel was the most softly spoken guy with a really delicate way of making me feel great about my work. His criticism was so covert that it took about half-an-hour for you to realize he'd even made it. Whilst he asked me questions about the drawing tendencies I couldn't seem to break, Bill had opened my drawer and pulled out a drawing that I kind of liked but hadn't deemed fit for my portfolio. The piece was a very vibrant and loose life drawing on an A1 sheet of cartridge paper.

Bypassing formalities, he placed his glasses on the drawers and burst into a machine gun hiss of foul language that I had never before encountered from any tutor. He told me in no uncertain terms that my life drawing works were the creative direction in which I needed to be heading in and that the stifled illustrations produced to date were poor in comparison.

Bill spotted the antagonistic side of my sense of humour and he must have trusted that I could take the heat of such fierce criticism. I might just respond better to this than the gentle coaxing reserved for quieter students. He could read people and teach in a manner that drew the best out of a person. That's what a good teacher does. He handed me my first ever set of decent acrylic paints, the ones you can't afford as a student, and told me that he knew I would put them to good use; that they were mine to keep.

I was unsure about the quality of the resultant piece, but when the two tutors returned 20 minutes later, they high-fived each other and warned me that if I ever looked back from this creative breakthrough, I would wish I hadn't. Despite my reservations, that project earned me my first distinction, the highest grade on offer in a BTEC. I had just been force-fed the first crumbs of my natural creative style.

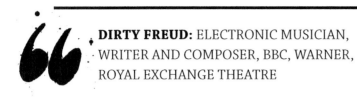

DIRTY FREUD: ELECTRONIC MUSICIAN, WRITER AND COMPOSER, BBC, WARNER, ROYAL EXCHANGE THEATRE

'I first got into music through my dad. He'd bring home all these wildly different vinyl records, be they psychedelic, reggae, hip-hop, 1980s swing. My mum was a roadie for Iron Maiden, and she was like, 'I'm not having this. All this musical influence from him and none from me…' so she started bringing home tracks like Def Leppard, Iron Maiden and lots of other heavier stuff. She took me on tour with them in the school holidays.

I've always been into the lyrical side of music, so I decided I wanted to write poetry and plays, which is how I ended up with a creative writing degree and not on a music course.

I remember expressing a desire to study and make music, so I approached my GCSE tutor. When he asked me what kind of music, I pulled out a Gary Numan CD that I had stolen from my mum, unbeknownst to her. He looked at me and told me that it wasn't 'real music,' because it was industrial, fresh and a little bit dirty and not classical or popular. Unfortunately, at 16, these things affect you because there is no capacity for critical thinking when you're a kid. You rely upon the experienced people to develop raw talent, so from then on, it was, 'Good, didn't want to do music anyway… next.' When I started to realize that maybe this was just his opinion, it was too late. Without my GCSE, they wouldn't let me on the A-level, so I opted for a career in writing.'

THE THING WITH DAMON ALBARN...

Throughout college, several of my obsessive personal interests took on a new relevance. I could now afford to watch Leeds United thanks to my part-time supermarket job. I never got the whole grunge music scene and Blur came into my life by way of lyrics that resonated with my small town teenage experiences. I'd be sat in front of Top Of The Pops on Friday nights, mesmerized by Albarn owning the stage, everything I could never be in the classroom, though it didn't stop me day-dreaming about winning over the popular girls at school in frontman fashion. He seemed to be from a galaxy far far away, certainly not from my planet; a demi-god enveloped by shoals of real-life girls and Harrington jackets that they didn't sell in Keighley.

I was too young to go out and *live* the combined explosion of the Young British Artists movement and great fresh British music infiltrating the radio stations and TV channels, which I now regard as a healthy thing, but my love of that band became the reason I would continue to draw. They simply inspired me creatively like little else did.

Music and art have always gone hand-in-hand. I was intrigued by that relationship. Record sleeve designs probably appeared in 90% of creative student's portfolios, but I persisted with my own efforts anyway. During college, Albarn started his musical side project, Gorillaz. I was enthralled by this multimedia marriage of the tunes and comic book illustrator Jamie Hewlett's character creations, animated so succinctly.

The tutors at college would drift around the studio and drop in for little one-to-one chats if you made eye contact or if you'd been avoiding them for too long. I mentioned to Bill that I loved Gorillaz and battered him with questions about the mechanics of animation. He would reference it every time I saw him in the building corridors and he bought the album, which made him the coolest tutor I had ever known, so I worked harder, desperate to impress him. From that point on I wanted to collaborate with musicians in the same way Hewlett and Albarn teamed up. My family home didn't have the internet yet, and we were only at the college computers for a couple of hours each week, so with very few musicians in Keighley and no way of reaching out to those further afield, I was restricted to mocking up alternate Blur sleeves as college projects in my suburban bubble. Like wrestling, I thought this creative man crush was something I'd soon grow out of. It wasn't.

MEN IN TIGHTS

I love professional wrestling. Laugh now and get it out of the way, but my cards are on the table. Shedding my inhibitions at college, I fell back in love with WWE and WCW, the two main televised wrestling promotions. My parents hadn't been able to afford Sky TV for a couple of years, so I was way behind in the storylines and new characters. My dad had a friend at work who had Sky, so with money from my supermarket part-time job, I would buy multi-packs of four-hour long VHS tapes and my dad would take them into work and ask him to record the pay-per-view events. I still don't know who the guy was, but it's a strange notion that he played a pivotal role in my career.

When my friends, my brother Sean and I had watched the events, I took the tapes home and designed my own covers with cut-out photos from *WWE Magazine* and gold marker pens when I should probably have been out trying to meet girls. They were appallingly bad, but I thought they were great at the time and that if the WWE ever saw them, I would be dragged out of college and placed straight in some sort of art worker role in their HQ over in the US.

The larger-than-life characters that make wrestling such a cultural anomaly have always fascinated me and their growing chokehold on my life quickly bled into my college work. Mask designs, colours of ring attire and mysterious back stories enthralled me and I started to paint giant A1-sized images of wrestlers, delivering their signature finishing moves. I had now started to love using a looser, messier style that benefited the subject matter. Bill pointed me in the direction of Peter Blake's early wrestling poster designs back in the 1950s.

My awareness of other artists and art history was, and still is, a weak point. I still used to throw folded bus tickets across the room at my peers' heads when the tutor's back was turned as they attempted to educate us about Art Deco, Andy Warhol or the Bauhaus movement. To ensnare my attention, something had to fall into *my world* in a context I understood. I think the art history sessions reminded me too much of school.

This revelation, that Blake had not only created the iconic sleeve for one of my favourite albums in *Sergeant Pepper's Lonely Hearts Club Band*, but also some seriously badass wrestling posters, had me all excited and I started to really develop the style that Nigel and Bill had excavated from somewhere within me. I was no longer scared to let the paint splats fall on my image or spray paint run down the sheet. I started going home looking like a painter and decorator.

By combining my pastimes and my education, a significant creative development had happened.

I worried about the effects of staying in my wrestling, football and Damon Albarn bubble. Other students would come up with these mind-blowing concepts. One friend made me insanely jealous by finding this vintage mannequin that he abandoned in a car park and then photographed each day charting its decay in a visual diary. His series of photographs made me feel like a child in comparison. He seemed exquisitely bohemian and arty so I started wearing jeans instead of the tracksuit bottoms I was still rocking.

What I hadn't grasped as a 17-year-old was that there was nothing wrong in obsessive focus. Until college, I had kept my drawings of wrestlers and footballers confined to the safety of my bedroom. Heaven forbid I should push the fruit bowl in art class to one side and replace it with a Hulk Hogan action figure from my backpack... revealing such geekiness just wasn't worth the verbal (and possible physical) beating that it would earn me. But now in this more adult environment where geeks were the dominant species, it was suddenly cool and encouraged to be a complete authority on something quirky.

Today, students email me and ask about my inspirations. I tell them it's all about what *you're* into. It has to be personal. At college, my paintings and my friend's mannequin were just our own ideas, products of our own experiences and interests. The passion that was central to both contrasting styles was mutual and we became friends. On college lunch breaks, I'd sit and wait for him to get his ears stretched at the body-piercing place, once a week he'd upsize. I didn't get it but I no longer mocked, just accepted it was *him*. Sometimes

I'd go to the newsagents and read the wrestling magazines for free until he was finished or I was asked to buy one or leave and that summed us up. Tom lived over in Leeds, had wild streaks of colour in his hair and listened to alternative bands. I hadn't yet explored the wider world, so I mapped out my bubble, with my Lego haircut. They were both fully valid traits, merely individuality, which is what the arts are about. I talked to him recently and we both admitted that back at college, we each felt that the other had everything perfected. It's now obvious that nobody did!

The only university taster I had experienced was a handful of trips to Leeds Metropolitan University to go to a comic fair they put on occasionally, in which I only saw the lobby and a few students wandering around with folders in their arms. Even that seemed daunting. It sounds ridiculous now, but at 17, I had yet to take the universe part of university as anything but literal. It felt like this other world where everyone was highly intelligent and knew about things like the galaxy and physics, something that I was only reading about in my comics below their dorms, wondering how the illustrators managed to draw so well. Bill looked gobsmacked when I told him I had no desire to go to uni and that I was considering applying for a job up the road, working on computer programmes for people with learning difficulties. He said we'd discuss this further at a later date. The frightening thing is, I meant it and I was crestfallen when the company said I really should go to university instead of joining them.

When I returned to college for my second year, people were already talking about university. Drawing was still drawing, painting still painting, so although I got that some of this stuff had commercial value, I had no idea how the skills I was exploring might be taken out of this college building and applied to the real world. Who was first point of contact? What would I say to them? How many others would be trying to reach them? How I would ever make money from it was another mystery entirely. I thought I'd better apply for something before I was left behind. I wasn't ready to get a full-time job. Everything seemed confusing when I picked up prospectuses. Fine art, to me, was really delicate, intricate drawing, where nothing could be mathematically incorrect, so I didn't even consider pursuing that path. In reality, fried eggs, dead cows in formaldehyde tanks and unmade beds had all fallen under that banner in recent years. I didn't know what anything meant or why the grinning students in the prospectus photos looked so happy, sitting on their single dorm beds, laughing so heartily, when I felt completely out of my depth, so I opted for the safest bet: graphic design.

What I learned

- Talent is crucial, but only part of the battle. People respond well to hard work and desire. They are more inclined to help those who are passionate and willing to listen and learn.

- You'll develop faster when you're interested in the creative working process and subject matter.

- It's ok to be obsessive, obsession is good when you use it creatively and professionally.

- Individuality is healthy, embrace it.

- Hangovers are destructive but conversations in the pub are productive, it's a tough balance to strike.

- The ability to talk to people is very valuable in the arts and crucial in freelancing, but don't talk nonsense or promise things you can't deliver, word gets around.

- A good tutor will know how to encourage and develop different personalities.

KEN GARLAND, BRITISH GRAPHIC DESIGNER AND AUTHOR OF *'THE FIRST THINGS FIRST MANIFESTO'*

'Out of my sister and I, I was the one who would always be drawing. I was going to do something in art. I also showed some promise in academic subjects. I was regarded with scorn by the grammar school teachers, because I wasn't prepared to go for a county scholarship and then apply for Oxford or Cambridge University. They thought I was wasting myself by going to art school. I have always resented that attitude. When I come across it subsequently – it still exists – I am very angry about it because I think it can lead people the wrong way. I told them to go and get f**ked. It may have been 'get stuffed,' at 16 but I had an absolute conviction that the thing these well-meaning people were telling me to do, was the very thing I should not do. Going to an art school was what I wanted to do. My parents supported me. They urged me to opt for commercial art so that I could earn a living. That's a very understandable attitude... There is still something in the background of our academic teaching that does not allow the teachers themselves to get their mind around the idea that going to an art school can be a really serious form of studying. They think it's just playing around, almost that it is a breeding ground for pop groups and nothing to do with serious study. That being said, it is feasible that one could go to art school and immerse one's self in art and design, neglecting the wider study of film, music and drama and I've always felt anxious that people who went to art school should be given a wider education.'

CHAPTER 3. STARTING UNIVERSITY

University was nothing to do with planets or meteor showers unless you'd chosen that subject.

I was accepted on the BA Honours degree course in graphic media communication at Bradford College in summer 2002. Some friends went off to places like Newcastle and London, others stayed relatively local. Ever since college, I'd started to surround myself with the broadest range of weird people I could find. I use that term in a very complimentary way. Pubs invariably provided plenty of them, with whom to align myself. I remember making one friend because he would go out for a beer after work and wake up behind billboards in Bradford with no idea how he got there. He once removed, and took home, a double bus seat without the driver noticing, so I asked for his phone number. I stopped caring what people thought of me, which really aided my creative work and the ideas that drove it, something I hoped university would further develop.

Despite being on a course that gave me a taste of lots of disciplines, I only wanted to draw and make images from photographs. I really hated the graphic design modules where we were taught the rules of layout and typography.

It was at college that an important mentality shift started to happen in the form of film. The course at Bradford contained a regular writing module, of which I hated the very mention when we were first told about it. Given that I had done very little academic writing, or any writing for that matter, since leaving school two years previously, I assumed, quite naively, that it would be painstakingly dull. But in reality, the idea was that here, we would learn to think critically about media forms, challenge things, break down art that interested us and look deeper than the surface of the finished product.

At this time, I had started a job at Blockbuster Video, part-time, outside of my study and I had started to take home movies that I would not normally watch. I became quite obsessed with the more innovative and challenging films. I was introduced to David Lynch's *Mulholland Drive*, David Fincher's *Fight Club* and indie cult classic, *Donnie Darko*. For the first time, I started to wonder how props were made and by whom? Who designed the movie posters? Maybe the original score and the visual feel of the film were not mutually exclusive. This way of thinking extended to the books I was reading, among other art forms. The writing module tutor allowed us to base our studies on anything creative that we chose, provided we met the course directives. It wouldn't occur to me for some time that, subconsciously, this heightened interest in wider media beyond wrestling, Blur and football was feeding my mind rich creative new fuel for my artistic output.

I hadn't been at Bradford college long when I started to grow restless and a bit disenchanted. My girlfriend at the time had applied for university courses further afield and seemed excited by the looming independence that moving away from home would bring. It made sense and I started to wonder why I had not left home. Every Friday, I was the small town champion, greeted by the cheers of my king's court upon walking through pub doors, something that had been enlightening at college, but now started to feel repetitive. Still being in my hometown when everyone had sailed off to the magical kingdoms of Keele and Huddersfield, where Champagne elixirs flowed and vixens swooned over artists, was unsettling me.

BUT IS IT ART?

School teaching was mainly about textbooks and facts and instilled in me the belief that teachers are omnipotent. I assumed that they were still the law at university; since the college tutors had got everything right, in my case, I had no reason to believe otherwise. While guidance and experience are invaluable and should be sought out, no matter what level you reach, I was about to learn that tutors on creative courses are also just part of the same crazy art world, where anything is built on personal perception.

It's staggering how many students, myself included, believe complexity and detail are essential for creative output to be considered good quality. Simplicity is the hardest thing to pull off. A five-second scribble can be just as legitimate as a painting that took four years to complete depending on its contextual setting, audience and role in a bigger picture. I had accumulated a shoebox full of poor quality disposable camera photographs from drunken college nights out over the last two years and I was determined to use them in some college project. I've always had a photographic memory for things that make me laugh, so I decided I was going to create a photo journal full of these images, write some amusing quotes gleaned from those nights over the top of them and call it 'Smashed.'

The three course leaders sat down to critique the project's final results. It was always quite a daunting experience, especially when I knew I hadn't worked very hard. I just hoped that my mock enthusiasm would be good enough to convince them otherwise.

At university level, the tutors were a little less forgiving than at college. I got up and presented my unfinished, badly presented journal full of photographs of drunken 17-and-18-year-olds rolling around on wet West Yorkshire pavements and jumping in bushes. One image depicted a concussed friend inside a public litter bin, rolling down a sloped pavement. A few giggles quickly subsided when the course leader put his head in his hands. One of those false laughs of despair and exasperation escaped him and he proceeded to tell me that I was capable of so much more and that this was the artistic equivalent of *The Daily Sport* newspaper's place in journalism. He said it was cheap, badly produced and lazy. It was a fierce damning and although I'd always taken criticism positively, I felt like I'd f**ked up my big opportunity in higher education. This wasn't constructive feedback, more of a stern warning to get my shit together. He was about to offer his suggestions for how I was to address this and give me the chance to rescue the project with a deadline extension when the second tutor interjected.

He apologized to the course leader and, although he felt that the journal could have been presented much more dynamically, couldn't agree that the idea was anything but a brilliant one and the photographs were extremely appealing for their lack of quality control. He said that although, on the surface, they were no different from any other photographs from any night out in the UK, the love for the images was evident in their considered composition and sheer quantity. He felt the way I had attempted to create rich characters from bricklayers, electricians and intoxicated students showed real creativity, attention to detail and a willingness to get under the skin of something that was, on the surface, quite mundane and common. To say I was shocked was an understatement. The tension between the two tutors was now thick in the air, like the *post mortem* atmosphere of a parental row. Everyone in the room was shifting awkwardly in their seats and suddenly I felt like I was the defendant in some sort of creative court.

The third tutor, the power player in this scenario, given his deciding vote, chose to sit on the fence. He said he couldn't work out whether it was genius or 'complete dog shit'. The rift my work caused amongst the faculty staff opened my eyes and suddenly I got it, this was a revelation. Not everything had to be a Renaissance tapestry to be good or interesting. I started to understand why the Young British Artists Movement had put art back at the centre of British popular culture in the 1990s. It was disgusting, sexy, awful and brilliant and, more importantly, *everyone* had an opinion on it. Something exploded in my head after the creative jury failed to reach a verdict and I had to find somewhere to let it all out where they'd just let me explore drawing and painting all day.

ILLUSTRATION (BA HONS)

I burst through the door of the design department at the University Of Central Lancashire, panicked and late for my interview after getting lost in town. Despite my slapstick arrival in Lancashire, and the fact that I had no idea what the discipline of illustration really entailed, Steve Wilkin, the course leader, saw enough in my portfolio and the funny side of the state of the sweaty, hyperventilating clown opposite him, to offer me a place on the BA Honours degree in illustration. I had to research it and found out that illustration was essentially image-making, often commissioned for editorial publications, children's literature and advertising. That seemed a bit more likely to lead to a career than fine art, given its commercial versatility. Steve had taught at Bradford College years earlier and supported Leeds United. That double connection gave us some crucial common ground and that made up my mind, along with a three-minute long interview at Leeds Metropolitan University, my only other option, in which the lady running the course grunted that my portfolio was a bit thin and told me that Preston would serve me better.

I lost my head completely in the first few days of university. The vixens and Champagne were nowhere to be seen and I couldn't sleep for the noise of drunken girls running around the corridors, slamming doors and vomiting in the bushes outside my window. I went back to Keighley over the first weekend to sleep for 16 hours straight and think about what I'd done. Returning with a new resolve, I gradually adapted to university life.

College had taught techniques and practical skills but the illustration course led with conceptual and creative thinking. I'd be lying if I said I loved the degree to begin with. I did what I had to do to pass my first year. I turned up, which was more than some students managed, but my strongest work remained in my BTEC portfolio from Keighley. I found students who seemed happy to rack up £10,000 of debt to sit there, do a few half-arsed drawings and then moan about the tutors not telling them what to do, infuriating. I realized that, from here on, the responsibility to make the most of this opportunity was resting on us. No spoon-feeding or else you'd learn nothing.

They had us doing a short course alongside the degree, which they called 'electives' where they encouraged us to broaden our cultural horizons. I was so annoyed by this that I reused an old piece from my college BTEC to pass it, pretending it was hot off the press. I was yet to consciously explore lands beyond the confines of art and design for creative inspiration and didn't get why they made it compulsory to do so. I had a lot to learn. It was not an easy thing for me to grasp and my first semester was spent learning why it is unhealthy to box yourself in by doing the same things all the time; mimicking Ralph Steadman's artistic style, in my case.

I needed to earn some money for my second year so my dad found me a job at Damart for the summer. Damart,where my dad had worked for years, was a household goods company in a small town called Steeton. I hated that job.

Every day I unloaded arctic trucks full of heavy boxes and wrote out stickers on corresponding crates in the warehouse. I had a massive attitude shift and I started to view my degree as an opportunity, one that my dad's selfless graft in this job for many years had given me. University could not become the socially acceptable context for going down the pub in the afternoon and evading employment.

There is nothing wrong with a manual job. My dad did his well and didn't mind it at all. It just isn't very good for a creative mind to be doing something repetitive for too long. I would come home in the evenings and batter my sketchbook with inks and spray paints which I'd bought with my summer wages. I started to peel the stickers from the boxes at work and use them as a starting point in artworks, I worked up ink drawings of quite dark characters, influenced by the negativity that was abundant at Damart. Drawing upon surroundings like this, using negative situations for positive creative output, was a new breakthrough. I was having a moan about how slowly the day was going one afternoon when a guy my age told me to shut up. 'It's alright you moaning, pal, but you get to go back to college or whatever in September, think about us lifers.' He spoke like it was a prison, but I realized that, with a negative mindset like that, he would be locked in for life. I told him he could leave at any time, but he called me a 'bloody student' and walked off grumbling at his trolley. I worked until 2am when I got home that evening. My future was in my hands. You can't coast through university and hope to avoid jobs that wear you down.

Sean, my brother, was a hero. He had convinced my folks to get Sky TV and he would record all WWE programming and send down three VHS tapes full of flagship shows (Raw, Smackdown and the pay-per-view events) to me in the post, using stamps that my dad had amassed from the 'goods-in' area at Damart.

Wrestling and football continued to influence my work in my second year without me consciously noticing, and the course became more vocational. We were set short deadlines on editorial illustration briefs. I enjoyed the challenge of thinking laterally, at speed, and thought this could be cool to do for a living. What the tutors tried to drum into me during the second and third years was the importance of trial and error, learning various techniques by accident.

But students can be stubborn and it would be a few more years before I realized they were right all along. It's so important that you enjoy your working process, no matter what you're doing. Can you imagine being an actor and hating people seeing you on camera or on stage? It's no different when you're picking up a paint-brush. If you don't like it, try loads of other mediums until you learn what works for you. It sounds simple, but degrees and even the arts, are full of people restricting themselves to one discipline, who stick to what they've been doing because they're scared to change direction, even though they might not be particularly enjoying that one thing.

The common belief that you have to find a distinctive 'signature style' of working before you graduate is misguided. We were all starting to learn that one of the most fundamental differences between graphic design and illustration was that illustrators were chosen because their recognizable creative style was right for a job, while designers were expected to be diverse and versatile. This started to make a lot of folk panic. What happens is, somewhere between second and third year, the fun is supplanted by the fear that you will fail and be condemned to a horrible death because you have not yet found your own signature style, when the only way to find it is to have the fun you just abandoned. It's a 'Catch-22 'and some people ended up quitting the degree because of the frustration it brings at a fragile time. I was finding it hard, but I just wanted my scroll and a shot at the industry by the time I started my final year. I couldn't wait to get out and into the marketplace.

We had just started to listen to visiting speakers as part of the professional practice modules they put you through to try and give you an idea of the life to which you're about to commit. Most of the speakers came across as gentle souls. I took a lot from their words and seeing the stuff we were producing now, in its real world context, changed everything, though the only speaker to whom I could really relate on a personal level was David Hughes, a top-level illustrator. I had doubted that someone from my small town background, who wasn't all that bohemian, would ever make it in the art world until I met him. David Hughes was a big personality and I took an instant shine to him in a passing encounter. He reminded me that the arts are riddled with all kinds of personalities.

It was the annual national Big Draw event. Hughes was a friend of course leader Steve Wilkin, and was taking the class. He had his own book out in the shops, full of portraits of famous people in his unmistakable style, and was my new favourite person. They had us drawing self-portraits in charcoal on massive sheets of paper, while Hughes and other staff members wandered about offering feedback. He took one look at charcoal-drawn me. 'F**k me, is your nose really that bent?' Looking me in the eye as I crouched there, on the floor, on all fours, staring back at him, he followed up: 'Wow, it really is, isn't it?'

University equipped us, as much as is possible, for the real world – but no one can be protected from what awaits after seven years of tutorial steering comes to a close. There's no utility belt full of gadgets to escape the trials awaiting you. You have to surround yourself with interesting people and learn to love the fight. In the second year at university, we were downsized to a studio that contained the final year students, the ones who would soon walk-the-plank and fall off the edge of student Eden, into tax-paying Hades.

One of the people who stood out was Danny Allison. I was aware of him simply because he'd constantly shout 'flange!' in the most ridiculous voice at a girl called Angela, making him unignorable to anyone on the whole corridor. He made me laugh straight away, though others wanted to punch him. I started to notice that certain artistic styles represent a personality. In my first year's Ralph Steadman-cloning efforts, I began to understand that a natural creative style has to become an extension of the personality behind it. That is one fact in a world in which there are not too many certainties. I saw the originality in Danny's work, understood the connection and allowed my humour to start creeping into my own work. To imitate is to disappear into a shadow of mediocrity. I was still discovering the early stages of my natural style when I met Danny. His illustrations, much like mine, were laborious and multi-layered. He dirtied it up, allowed mistakes to breathe and his concepts were clear and clever. I envied him for this. Just when I thought we might become friends, he was gone.

REAL WORLD INCOMING

Education ended unceremoniously. A break-up with the girl I was seeing was followed by almost getting punched in the head by another girl on my course. People were starting to ask all those awful questions that you hear when you're starting out as an artist. 'Any money in that?'; 'What if you can't find any work?'; 'Can't you get a proper job?'; 'Ah I get that you're an artist, but what do you *do?*'

The reason a girl wanted to punch my head in was no different to the reason the school teacher made me design the dyslexia poster: I had drawn them both in a distinctly offensive manner. We were planning the new graduate exhibition in which we would showcase our degree show work - the best of the past two years. My friend and course mate had stuck his neck out for all of us and paid the hostel deposit from his student loan and here he was, taking this public dressing-down from a girl who was pissed off we wouldn't be staying at a hotel. I'm no good at confrontation, so I opened my sketchbook and drew her, really quite lifelike as far down as the arse, which I enlarged out of all proportion, added an unnecessary thatch of hair to it and dropped a huge marker pen penis onto her forehead.

It was intended to make my friend laugh when we got home but I remembered I'd left my pen drive in the computer room, hanging out of one of the Macs with my exhibition prints on it and ran back to get it. When I returned, I walked back into crackling silence. The girl who had pissed me off was now stood eyeballing me with a bright red face, trembling and waving the finger at me. She had found the drawing on my desk.

'Did I really piss you off *so* much that you had to bully me? This is a personal assault and it's unforgivable Tallon, you bastard!' I can't recall the rest, but I just covered my head with both hands in the way you do when a large dog is stood on its back legs trying to lick your mouth, or a boxing instructor is testing your defensive skills. Course leader, Steve, who is not the tallest guy, had to stand in between us and ask me to wait outside in the corridor while he diffused the situation. A fortnight before I was about to make my parents all proud in my cap and gown I was being sent out of class, a child to the very last days of my education.

VICTORIA PEARCE: FORMER FASHION AND PHOTOGRAPHY AGENT, CURRENT AGENT AT ILLUSTRATION LTD

'After getting the three O-levels I focused on, I studied on a BTEC in fashion design at Cheltenham College of Art from 1986-88 and then a four-year sandwich degree in Newcastle in fashion design and marketing. A large part of the reason I then went to university in Newcastle was because of the scene up there at the time. In one of my student flats, I collaged the kitchen with pictures, cut out from The Face and I-D.

After my degree, I moved down to London without really knowing what I wanted to do. The course I had done was very commercially-orientated. So when we'd designed a range, set to a brief, we'd be asked to think about who it was going to be aimed at, how would we market it? Had we done the research? I thought, 'Oh no, this is going to be really restrictive, blah blah blah', but it was fantastic for learning how to apply your work commercially.

When I graduated, it was 1992 and the recession had just hit, so there were limited opportunities for graduates. I managed to get a job working for a photographic agent as a junior booker. It was a big studio complex in King's Cross called 'The Worx' and it all fell into my lap. The agent represented fashion photographers, so it was in the heart of the world in which I had aspired to work in pre-college; work that is created and ends up on a magazine page. I loved that role, working with a wide range of creatives, stylists, hair and make-up artists, set designers, booking models, organising a huge crew all to come up with a final image.

I then went to work for a design consultancy called Studio M for three years. Suddenly I was on the other side of the table and we had the contract to do all of the fashion shoots for BHS, which was a big account, also FHM's fashion content. My role was managing the production and overseeing the whole creative crew. That was at the height of the lads' mag culture. We would be booking a whole range of freelance photographers. We had shoots in the Bahamas, Miami, all over the world and the art director was the kind of guy who would throw you in at the deep end, putting faith in you. I had to learn a lot about technology and film on the job, as it was all pre-digital. You are essentially the interface between the client and the team, so the guys we'd use on the shoot were not just chosen for their skills; but personality and ability to be a team player was just as important. If you're going on a shoot for longer periods, you have to get along. You're not just working with the crew, but also dining and socialising with them.'

GRAPHIC ACTIVISM

Besides editorial illustration and drawing wrestlers, I had developed an interest in graphic activism and decided I would write about it in my degree dissertation. I had finally stumbled upon a better outlet for my inner antagonist than drawing genitals on people's heads. I discovered Bristol graffiti artist Banksy in Sainsbury's on the sleeve of Blur's *Think Tank* album, just after being dumped in the supermarket carpark by a girl I'd dated in the first year at uni. I decided to investigate this type of social commentary in design further. A wider group of unthinkably cool artists like Blek Le Rat, Ken Garland and Jonathan Barnbrook all revealed themselves to me, people who also challenged existing ideas through their creative work.

Ken Garland had rounded up a group of artists who pledged their free time to *The First Things First Manifesto* in 1964 – a bill that stated all enlisted would turn their talents to things they believed would benefit society instead of the commercial, soulless race for riches. Ken was, and still is, a Campaign for Nuclear Disarmament (CND) activist and he supported them with his skills. He also did some slick design for Galt, a company which manufactured educational toys for children. It wasn't all about going on the offensive, more a carefully focused, benevolent utilization of creative energy.

The press featured the manifesto heavily and attention in the arts was plentiful. (I loved the idea of seeing myself featured in anything at all; even the university newspaper would do). Jonathan Barnbrook had followed Garland's lead in heading *The First Things First Manifesto in 2000*, rekindling the idea with a new group of artists 36 years later. I thought these guys created something to which I could aspire and I began thinking more critically about the things around me. I had no idea how to influence or change anything on my own; I was, and still am, a political novice. Here were visual blueprints I could study that might show me an alternative way to influence many people. I graduated with a 2:1 honours degree in illustration. It was a decent grade but I felt nowhere near where I wanted to be in terms of style.

The *New Blood* exhibition was my first trip to London in more than a decade and it felt, simultaneously, like the end of one world and the birth of a whole new galaxy in my head. It opened my eyes to the sheer quantity of creative brilliance that the UK produces and I was aware that the market was by now, truly global, thanks to the internet. It was inspiring and sobering. I was literally up against the world, or so it seemed. I thought my university work was sublime until I walked into that place. Now I was looking at row after row, wall after wall of high quality work that blew mine out of the water in one of the most culturally vibrant cities on the planet.

Chinese whispers were telling us that someone from Liverpool had spoken to a *real* art director, *from London* no less. A girl from Camberwell was rumoured to have sold a piece and was now being considered for a commission. I heard one drunken Geordie telling his mate he might try to kiss one of the organizers (just before he fell into the partition wall, smashing one of his pieces and some champagne flutes).

Commissions and art directors were things I had only heard mentioned in talks; mythical Titans that only the enlightened got to see and experience. Despite knowing that he was right, given his experience as course leader, I made excuses when course leader Steve Wilkin suggested I should call some magazines and go and show them my portfolio and went to the pub with my class and got pissed to drown out the noise of worrying. None of us even managed merriment, we had been well and truly sobered up by the glimpse of what stood before us. Education's protective shield had been confiscated and things would not be the same again.

- Shedding inhibitions can aid creative thinking and progression.

- Tutors can be wrong, like everyone else. Pay attention all the same, because experience is priceless and their opinions are more informed than a student's.

- University is not a fairytale land. The girls get very drunk and sometimes their skirts get caught in their tights.

- Nobody holds your hand at university; you chose to attend. You're an adult and have to be self-motivated to get something out of it.

- People with industry experience can teach you a lot, get in touch with them. Break down doors if you have to.

- Do not rely on the arts for creative fuel and inspiration, fill your head with new places and ideas.

- Repetitive employment is not good for the creative brain but can finance the long game and teach you things. Use the shit jobs to good effect and do not get trapped or downbeat.

- Concentrating on enjoying your studies will bring better results than labouring over what you think the tutors want to see.

- There is a place for absolutely everyone in the arts, find yours and own it.

- Your natural style is a product of your environment, be yourself and draw on your humour, quirks, background and differences.

- Mimicry is a fast track to anonymity.

- Creativity is a great channel for venting negative emotions. Grab your frustrations and turn them into silver linings.

✦KEN GARLAND, GRAPHIC DESIGNER,
ON *'THE FIRST THINGS FIRST MANIFESTO'*, 1964

'My manifesto was not about benevolent design, but more about the misappropriation of public wealth. I believed that we had a huge amount of surplus wealth, created by the workers, which had gone into the pockets of people who were misapplying it. A lot of the time and skills of people like us (designers, photographers and artists) were being misused because the funds had been distorted. People who were manipulating huge amounts of funds didn't deserve the wealth or know how to use it. I wanted it better used.

It was never an ethical decision, more a political one. I was basically talking socialism in design. This turned itself, in people's interpretation of the manifesto, into me being 'Mr Ethics', which I wasn't. We all have our ethics and morals, even the villains with their distorted ideas. Historically, there is always this body of opinion that says our skills have to be applied to the right subject, for the right cause. I support causes, obviously. I wouldn't be wearing a CND (Campaign for Nuclear Disarmament) badge if I didn't support that cause and others. But I still maintain that what I was, and still am, talking about is what we do with our surplus wealth. That's kind of odd now because surplus wealth has almost disappeared. The bloody bankers have gone and squandered it. Now we have to build it all over again.'

CHAPTER 4. WELCOME TO FREELANCING

There's this overnight changeover that happens immediately after you've thrown your hat in the air during the graduation ceremony. Nothing feels that different; you're most likely still broke and many familiar faces are still in town, but your status switches emphatically from student to unemployed and the psychological impact of that is not to be underestimated. Drinking in the afternoon is no longer acceptable without the social camouflage with which higher education shrouds you.

I managed to turn my weekend job at Waterstones bookstore into a full-time 8.30-5pm gig. This meant I switched from manning the tills, dealing with customers upstairs to unpacking boxes of books in the goods-in department, a cold basement under the shop. It alleviated the financial pressure somewhat, but I felt the hot breath of my inner voice, whispering to me, telling me I was not making any creative progress in this job. But what alternative did I have without a student loan? This was the first time in my life that I'd had to worry about rent and council tax.

Waterstones was a good gig. The company looked after their staff more than most employers for whom I had previously worked and the staff roster included many creative people. I shared the role with a guy who had done the goods-in job for a few years. His dry sense of humour made it enjoyable for the most part. You'll find artistic worth in absolutely anything if you look for it and that place was full of interesting members of staff. Everyone seemed to be chasing a dream or on the way back from one. Some of the friendships I made in that job brought great support and encouragement at a time when I really needed it. At this point, I wasn't quite seeing the long-term positives that having a full-time job to finance your passion provides. That way of thinking would take a few more years to develop.

I set myself what I felt was a realistic goal: to be self-employed and illustrating full-time when Euro 2008 came around two years later, so that I would not have to worry about pulling sick days to watch the England football matches. I bought a £20 garden table, dragged the spare kitchen chair upstairs and stuck a photo of Damon Albarn on the wall, who was now four years departed from Blur, but no less musically active and still inspiring me. This would be my office and I attempted to start crafting a portfolio that was better than embarrassing.

The changeover from full-time education to working on my artwork on top of my full-time job was incredibly hard going. I lived with two of my fellow illustration graduates and friends who were in the same boat, adrift on the sea of sobering transition. We all lacked any sort of healthy pressure to do new work now that we had no external authority to satisfy. The biggest thing that was missing was someone more experienced than us to provide critical feedback about our work. I found myself not only struggling to produce anything of any merit, but floundering completely.

I had reverted back to college standards, seemingly overnight. Self-confidence dipped alarmingly and I found myself doing anything other than illustrating. I started watching even more wrestling, I got into reading strange books, like one detailing all the possible doomsday scenarios that a friend had picked up and brought round to the house. He found it funny, knowing fine well that my morbid curiosity would compel me to read it, and I almost sent myself into a state of mental disrepair. I have this bizarre fascination with horror films and assorted weirdness, which I cannot ignore, despite the fact my imagination runs riot and unravels me completely. It's the reason I've never touched hallucinogenic drugs.

Creative minds are ethereal and unpredictable places, beautiful and rippling with great intent, but full of trap doors to pits of stupidity and needless worrying and I did a lot of that, mainly about my career prospects during my Waterstones days. The lack of customers, now supplanted by trolleys full of books which couldn't complain or ask me where the popular science section was situated meant I was left with too much thinking time on my hands.

The old Apple desktop computer I had bought from a colleague at Waterstones had none of the programmes I required to complete my illustrations and a month later, stopped working altogether. I would draw portraits using pen and ink or have a go at self-initiating an editorial illustration brief, but it was dire and I could not finish them, since my working process required a computer. I became quite downhearted about my prospects.

Despite seven years in education, I realized I had no clue how to make a decent living as an artist. I kind of grasped that an art director or art editor was the person at a print publication who I needed to contact for work. They were responsible for sourcing all images used in a magazine or newspaper, whether that was buying the rights to use a stock photograph or commissioning a full page or front cover illustration. I knew that illustration was often used in advertising, but I had no way of knowing if the people I had to contact to get editorial work would have the same job title in advertising agencies. What was the difference between the art director and the creative director? Why do theatres insist on the full extended title, 'artistic director?' is that pomposity or practical sensibility? How fine artists made any kind of living selling ceramic vaginas or traditional canvas paintings was a riddle to me. Let's face it, that's a pretty niche market.

Some of the graphic designers told me they had jobs lined up from their university placement employers whom they had impressed. I envied them quite a lot. One lad started on a £25,000 salary the week after graduation while the closest I was getting to the art world was through the pages of the books I was arranging and sending up two floors. Had I chosen the wrong degree? Was I becoming the classic person qualified to high heaven, but unable to get a gig at the local hardware store? These questions kept me awake into the early hours. I figured that soon, I would send some sample work to a selection of magazines and take it from there. Soon... Aside from getting a gig as an artworker at some greeting cards company, it was the only realistic starting point I could see.

I started to feel I had exhausted the value of my job at Waterstones. I had no interest in progressing with the company and my heart was in the creative industries. During lunch breaks at work, I'd eat my packed lunch as soon as possible and head for the art and design corner of the store to flick through the creative compendiums. Each page slapped my snivelling face with a beautiful, distinctly-styled image on heavy gloss stock. I wanted this lifestyle so urgently, but it felt detached, so far away because I wasn't doing anything creative to further myself or earn it. That garden table office was gathering dust.

SAM PRICE: FREELANCE ART DIRECTOR, *TOP GEAR* MAGAZINE, *MATCH OF THE DAY* MAGAZINE, Q MAGAZINE, *BIG ISSUE* (ART DIRECTOR 2007-2011)

'I sleep better now, since going freelance. In magazine work, on a day rate, you're temporary, so you don't have to worry about it too much. When you're not connected anymore, you do your hours and you go home, nothing more, nothing less. It's measured out in pages and days. Ownership is less. The freedom is more in a way, but it's frustrating when you can see the problem, but carry no power to address it. You still have a say but there's less politics. If you make a mistake, you get told the same day. At the Big Issue, when you're part of the core team, it comes back three or four weeks later and you're responsible. The dialogue wasn't good. When you freelance, you essentially have to please one person, but before, there was company pressure.'

IT'S WHO YOU KNOW...

That old expression, 'It's who you know, not what you know' is kind of true. But what you have to ask is how do you *get* to know these people? You're not just handed a network, you have to work for that and people have to like you and what you do. Time, patience, money, effort, personality and *what* you know is also important, so don't be fooled. I graduated with an empty database.

Rich Taylor had graduated in the same year as me, from the furniture design degree course. He was a friend of a friend and I finally met him in person after seeing him ghosting around the art department building a lot without ever getting the chance to say hello. Rich is the kind of person who is happier for you than you are for yourself when something good happens. You feel like you can tell him your filthiest secrets within an hour of meeting him. He had won an award for his chair design at university and he told me about a creative grant that was available through an initiative called 'Fresh Creative'. I was so impressed by his furniture design award and his beard that I took notice. I was just about covering my living costs with my full-time wage and my outlandishly ambitious football bets were not bearing any fruit, so I had no way of affording the £1,000 worth of Apple Mac that I needed simply to start creating my illustrations. I went to chat to the guys at Fresh Creative and told them Rich Taylor had sent me to see them.

Only one week earlier, I had threatened to quit art for good after the Apple Store had denied me a three-year credit plan on a Macbook laptop computer, due to my lack of debt, and therefore lack of credit rating. It felt crushing at the time but was quickly revealed as a blessing in disguise. I was assigned

Rich's friend, who steered me through the programme. She agreed with his opinion that my graduation portfolio was half decent. I instantly took a shine to her and we got along well. She walked me through six weeks of one–to-one consultation sessions in which they assisted me in writing a business plan, something I had not even heard of.

The process made me answer all the questions that forced me to think about things I had not considered, such as who my market was, how I would reach these people and what professional attributes set me apart from my competition. I looked forward to my mentoring sessions each week and the guys running the scheme believed I would be a strong candidate to be awarded some start-up money. They were right and I walked away with a bit of business direction, industry understanding and just shy of £1,500, a game-changing sum of money which I spent on a Macbook laptop, the programmes I needed to design things and some art materials.

To a creative person, that word, 'business,' can be like garlic to a vampire. I've witnessed some individuals quit at the very mention of the word. It was used a lot over the six weeks I spent on the Fresh Creative scheme. It doesn't matter how bohemian you are, how many abstract ideas are rippling through your works or how far you distance yourself from conventional ideas, the bottom line is: when you are paid to perform your skills, you are a operating a business, so you quickly have to start behaving like one in order to be taken seriously. The 'creative director of wherever' does not know that the rip in the left knee of your skinny jeans signifies your indomitable flair. She probably thinks you're a scruffy bastard who should not be trusted with a budget.

I took a trip down to my local tax office and registered as 'Ben and Ink Illustration', a title a friend had coined at university. I hated it from the off, it sounded like a pun, but it was memorable and nobody knew or cared who Ben Tallon was, so I stuck with it.

Some people talk about having a 'spirit guide', a guardian presence, invisible to the naked eye. Native Americans, birds of prey and wild cats are common visual associations, but in late 2006, Rich Taylor, a bloke the same age as me, from Chesterfield, was mine. I could see him too, walking in living colour on my earth. He rescued me from the bedroom garden table office at which I had been avoiding sitting, of late. He may as well have worn a cape, over the coming few months. He called one of my housemates one night as the two of us sat sketching at the kitchen table, to ask if the two of us had thought about renting a workspace. We hadn't. Two of his fellow furniture design graduates had stumbled upon an old stable that had previously been used as a car garage workshop. They needed two more people to take the cost down to £40 per head, per calendar month. I shrugged my shoulders and said: 'Count me in'. I figured that if I shaved a couple of pints off each night out, I suddenly had enough capital to rent the space.

My £40 per month bought me a freezing cold section of a garage just outside Moor Park in Preston: the Stables (named so because prior to being a car garage, the place was used as a stable for horses) It was a 45-minute walk from my house. Some nights, one of the lads who shared with us would drive up there and pick up me and my housemate, en route, but most times, we'd walk. It had no furniture, but upstairs was a little sink, toilet and a power supply that ensured we had the basics in place. We sorted out internet access and a phone line and the resident furniture designers cobbled together the most ridiculously-oversized desks for us. They were the size of 12-foot snooker tables and I had to crawl along the top of my desk to reach the pens and spray cans I lined along the back. It also meant that if I wanted to put in a proper shift, I had a makeshift bed that only required a duvet. It was really exciting and I wanted to spend all my time there. I remember sitting down with the four others and we each had ideas for collaborations and cool individual projects. We excitedly speed-talked, over rapidly cooling cups of tea. We were all in line for our industry thrones that night, anything felt possible.

At weekends, I would make the most of my time off from Waterstones by spending from 10am until 6 or 7pm in there before going out for beers. Some Sundays, I put in 15-hour stints from 8am until 11pm. Sometimes, if Rich was in, I'd go and sit in the corner when he was working and we'd just talk about everything that was ahead of us as designers. It was exhilarating. The camaraderie made everything feel conquerable, the turnaround from doing nothing, wasting my time in my bedroom was remarkable.

The kettle was our god in that place, a second-hand table became our tea-shrine.

There was a two-inch gap under the front door where the arctic swirls would breach the place and the only defence we had were halogen heaters so we had to layer up and rely on the pathetic bit of warmth we got out of them to counter the unholy chill. Despite the cold, I sometimes struggled to sleep from sheer excitement, a buzz I seldom feel as an adult, the same giddiness you felt when you were first allowed to stay at a friend's house or you had your first kiss.

The Stables awakened a passion I had thus far only felt for Leeds United, Blur and professional wrestling. All I wanted to do was create. I used to rush home from Waterstones, eat my tea to save money on buying food and then march all the way up to the office wearing three or four jumpers. Renting a workspace created a nice psychological divide between home and work. Sometimes, I didn't even have a plan for when I arrived. I just felt alive when I walked through the door and put on the kettle. This was what I'd been missing.

♦ROGER BROWNING: DESIGN DIRECTOR, *THE GUARDIAN* NEWSPAPER, 1995-2013

'Sometimes you need to use illustration, sometimes you don't. It varies from week to week. But most of the illustration we were commissioning was for the Saturday edition. Back before the recession, given the number of sections within the paper, it wasn't unusual for Sarah Habershon (art director, The Guardian) to commission two or three illustrations for the covers of the Work, Money and Family sections. For me, I'd regularly commission for the cover of review and stuff for inside; for Saturdays we would be commissioning six or seven reasonably big illustrations.'

FIRST COMMISSION

Sure enough, my first paid commission came through knowing someone who knew someone. Rich's then girlfriend, Sara, worked at a design collective in Manchester called Ultimate Holding Company (UHC). They positioned themselves as an ethical creative studio. Sara was aware of my work through my workspace with Rich and called to see if I was interested in creating an illustration to be used on the cover of *Enterprise Magazine*, a low-budget monthly publication about social enterprises. She told me they had £80 to spend as it was a not-for-profit company and asked if I could come over to chat about the brief. I was at home when I got the call. It remains the only time I have thrown a loaf of bread at the wall out of pleasure.

At the meeting they told me they loved the work in my portfolio, particularly these fairly dark characters I had made by cutting up photocopies of illustrated books about the human body. I just put the skeletal diagrams and muscular, skinless bodies back together again in a more interesting way and drew over the top.

They felt it was perfect for the feature on nursing. I came back with this twisted image of a big muscular head, with an arm coming out of the mouth, catching coins that had been dropped by a little nurse with only the diagram of a wide open mouth for a head. If you Google my name, I think it's still out there, somewhere. UHC loved it but the client went completely bananas when this gothic horrorscape landed on their desk and they cancelled the commission immediately, running instead with a really dull, out-of-focus photograph of a bald doctor forcing a smile. I was a little disappointed but I had learned a valuable basic lesson: always get the end client's approval before delivering final artwork. UHC had not floated the concept past the publisher before giving me the green light and there was no time to change the artwork before the magazine went to press. Thanks to my having behaved myself sufficiently to learn something during university professional practice modules, I had remembered to confirm the job in writing (a golden rule), so I still got paid, even if I did have to find out what a proper invoice was supposed to look like.

I had now landed my first commission, even if it never saw a printing press and I grew really restless at Waterstones. The job was still enjoyable for the most part, but now I'd had a taste of a career in the arts, I was hopelessly hooked and everything else immediately paled in comparison. Midway through one of my many impassioned speeches about my plans to rule the art world, which I would spew out to anyone who came downstairs at the shop, my Waterstones goods-in colleague cut me off and quietly asked me when I was going to stop talking about it and actually *do it*. He had worked with me enough to know how much my art meant to me and I think it had started to irk him that I had not yet left in wholehearted pursuit of it. His question stopped me dead in my tracks and I muttered something about doing it soon, when I could afford to quit my job.

When you've spent £950 of a £1500 overdraft, quitting your job and joining the dole queue isn't the most logical and informed call you can make, but it was the first of several instinctive, compulsive decisions that would have to be made to progress and I could not ignore my frustration any longer. I handed in my notice and left a fortnight later without a real plan.

What I learned

- Life after graduating is not easy. It's a culture shock, but don't despair; it's the beginning of exciting times if you're prepared to work for them.

- A degree is not a magnet for riches and fame, it is a foundation on which to build and that takes dedication and hard work.

- It is no longer socially acceptable to start drinking in the afternoon when you're not a student.

- Getting a full- or part-time job to support your passion, contrary to common artist folklore, is a good thing provided it serves your long-term goals.

- It takes time and costs money to start a business. Be patient and realistic, with a sprinkling of sacrifice.

- A garden table in a bedroom is not an ideal office, but can be made to work if you're disciplined enough.

- The cut off from years of tutorial input is difficult, surround yourself with people off whom you can bounce ideas. Ideally, hire an affordable external space to work from.

- If people pay you money to carry out a skill, you are a business, no matter how creative or arty that service is. Act like one.

- Business plans are not as evil as they seem. They force you to learn about your market. Write one.

- Be sociable and network yourself to death. People who know people are good people to know, but you have to meet them first.

- 'Spirit guides' can be from present day Chesterfield, or anywhere else. Do not overlook those already in your world as a source of help.

- A kettle is the heart of a small business. Take a moment and make a cup of tea in testing times.

- Always confirm any job in writing, with no exceptions. This is for your own protection. Don't blindly trust anybody, ever.

- Check the client is happy with your ideas before starting final artwork to avoid wasting time and effort.

VICTORIA PEARCE: FORMER FASHION AND PHOTOGRAPHY AGENT, CURRENT AGENT AT ILLUSTRATION LTD

'After working at Studio M, in 2000, I left and set up my own business with Eve Stoner. We were called Pearce-Stoner Associates, primarily representing fashion and advertising photographers and a couple of stylists, before moving into representing a couple of fashion illustrators, which eventually led me into the world of illustration.

Jacqueline Bissett, a fashion illustrator I met while at Studio M, approached me and asked if we'd be interested in representing an illustrator. She'd been illustrating for several years and had been independent to that point. I was very flattered that she asked and it occurred to me that we'd be marketing her to the same clients as our fashion photographers, so we agreed to work together on an experimental basis. We managed to get her work into new arenas and command fees that often, freelancers find it hard to ask for when they're solo.

Based on the success of representing Jackie, we took on some more fashion/contemporary illustrators: Natasha Law, Stephen Wilson, Daisy De Villeneuve, Neil Murren, Rose Stallard, Molly Molloy and David Downton among others. We developed and timed it well at a point when there was an interest in fashion illustration happening again. This also coincided with the rise of digital photography, forcing a lot of photographers to retrain digitally in order to survive.

Then the trend of digital retouching in photography began to happen and although it is amazing, it is total artifice. It happened at a time when I became a mother and had a young daughter. These models had a fantastic figure to start with, not to mention the best photographers and stylists, yet here they are, being hyper-airbrushed and it was starting to sit more and more uncomfortably with me as a parent.'

CHAPTER 5. SELF-UNEMPLOYMENT

My parents were worried that I had quit my job without any money to keep me going until I found something else, but beyond the odd inquisition on the phone, they trusted me enough to believe I could sort myself out.

Contrary to my calm reassurances on the phone to them, I was engulfed in financial paranoia. I spent the next month trying not to spend any money apart from on food, domestic bills and my Stables rent. I started going to the workshop for anywhere between 60 and 80 plus hours a week, sometimes more. I dragged planks of wood from nearby bin sites and painted on them, I created conceptual illustrations, textured backgrounds and all manner of crazy things. I managed to lure in the nearby garage's black-and-white mongrel dog at one point. It went mental, running all over the worktops and knocked over a pot of ink, which gave him some extra markings. I hoped his owner wouldn't be able to tell.

I was still battling with the half-formed style of image-making with which I had graduated. Creating the odd gem, like the unpublished magazine cover that was now at the front of my portfolio, helped me keep up spirits, but most of it still felt like a chore, which suggested that I had not yet found my natural style. I had my first set of promotional postcards printed, but it had escaped my attention that on the cards, there was nothing to direct the recipients to more work. I had no shop front to which my cards would direct potential clients. I needed a website. Starting marketing without one was a little bit stupid of me.

What little money I had left from my overdraft was running out far too quickly, but I spent it semi-wisely. I bought a *Dreamweaver For Dummies* book and a good supply of pens and paper. I had been given a free short course in Dreamweaver, one of the industry-standard website design programs, while at Keighley College, and with the book, I battled through the chapters, constructing the most basic, clumsy portfolio website you have ever seen. I sat there, for at least 12 hours each day, swearing at my laptop every time I messed up a piece of HTML code. To keep warm, I would sporadically run up and down the wooden staircase to the bathroom. I listened obsessively to Blur and Gorillaz, Albarn's other band, at full volume, while the others were out of the studio, at work in their day jobs, and kept my head down, grinding out the work to keep stress at arm's length.

I didn't have the money to pay a web designer so I would have to deal with a site build in this blood pressure-raising manner. Three quarters of the way through the build, I accidentally deleted some html code and had no idea how to replace it. I was on the verge of tears and almost broke my foot when I kicked a really heavy, mid 1990s monitor that I had scavenged from a nearby street and kept by the side of my desk, 'in case I ever needed it'. Despite the trials and rapidly dwindling finances, I somehow kept the faith long enough to go through the site build all over again. There it was; my very first website, my little corner of the art world where anyone could amble by and take a look. No matter how unlikely, absolutely anybody could now feasibly lay eyes on my work and that felt brilliant.

I found employment agencies to be hot-beds of incompetence, but a potential short-term means of affording to eat. On four separate occasions, inside a month, the agency in town had lost my CV after asking me to bring in a copy and showed no sign of pouring my increasingly sorry self back into the world of employment. I had made huge steps in my art career over the course of a month, sitting at my snooker table-sized desk in the Stables, but I didn't feel like a freelance professional, given the absence of paid work and my morale needed a lift with a sign I was doing the right thing. My CV would read that I had an 80-hour per week hobby if this website build was to be the pinnacle of my creative achievements.

Most people feel embarrassed about claiming benefits, but the reality is, you're only one misfortune away from requiring the financial crutch. If the employment agency was characterized by polite mistakes, going into the Job Centre office was one of the most soul-destroying 'career' experiences you'll ever go through, as a young British artist. It strengthens you no end, but what hurts is not your pride, (you quickly get over that) but the seemingly incompetent meat market system they run down there. I found myself passed from one member of staff to the next and they never seem to be able to find your records, so you have to start again with every visit. Every time I went, there seemed to be someone shouting and disorientated at 9am or aggressively kicking off with the staff. You'd see idiots coming out with their money and making a beeline straight for the Wetherspoons pub perfectly positioned right next door. The Stables made everything bearable and was my perfect shelter from all of this.

Around the one month self-unemployed mark, my money ran out. I had one, solitary, quivering pound left in my wallet, half a loaf of bread that would stretch to the end of the week if I kept it fastened tight and three-quarters of a bag of pasta at home. I was still determined not to phone home and ask for a loan to see me through so I spent the last pound to my name on a jar of economy peanut butter, which would work for both breakfast and lunch. I stopped outside the job centre, placed the jar on top of my bag while I arranged the various forms they had given me and watched desperately as the jar rolled off the top of my bag and smashed on the rain soaked floor. I tried to salvage it but the glass had splintered all over the place and into the butter. That was enough, my head gone, I called my mum and asked to borrow £20 to see out the week. Two days later, the agency called and said they had two days of work for me. At least it was something.

SAM PRICE: FREELANCE ART DIRECTOR, *TOP GEAR* MAGAZINE, *MATCH OF THE DAY* MAGAZINE, *Q* MAGAZINE, *BIG ISSUE* (ART DIRECTOR 2007-2011)

'I send out the curse email: 'I'm available on these days'. Then it's a waiting game. I've approached everyone myself so far. It's a 100% re-booking record apart from Haymarket Media. I have a day rate, so it's frustrating because if you're

fully freelance, you can jump on any level of project. With the day and hour rate ceiling, you can't always reach all levels.

The money is as good as when I was at the Big Issue, *but the freedom isn't there. That was mine. With this, I'm hired as a tool. It's good to work on quality products and see how they work. With* Match Of The Day Magazine, *for example. It's a nice thing to work with your heroes sometimes, and other times… it's not always so cool. You get the photos back from cover shoots and then come the demands. The retouching is ridiculous. I've had hairline regeneration demands from Hollywood A-Listers. We once had to make a major, major rapper's head more round, it was part of terms for him agreeing to be in the* Big Issue.*'*

TEMPORARY WORK

I arrived at The British Aerospace offices in Preston for my two days of temporary work in the least creased shirt my wardrobe had to offer. I felt safe in the knowledge that with my crappy little website online, I was out there in the creative world making up some ground I had lost in the six months after graduation. Having a website and a commission under my belt reinstated me as the invincible ruler of my world and made life's day-to-day trials just a little bit easier to deal with.

They sat me on reception at British Aerospace where my role was to hand out and collect various coloured pass cards that enabled the staff to access different areas of the building. In my mind, the top-level security areas were like the moon bases I'd seen on *Moonraker* and other *James Bond* films growing up. I wondered whether British Aerospace might play any part in the doomsday scenarios in my book? Was I creating a fantasy world to deal with these jobs? It was quite possible. I kept a pocket-sized sketchbook handy under the desk, making the most of gaps between staff arrivals. It wasn't too long before I noticed that the regular employees would hurry through reception, preoccupied with something seemingly really urgent, trying not to acknowledge the presence of the security guard in the booth opposite my desk. I've met a good few security guards and most of them seem to be completely unpredictable characters. He didn't seem to mind me doodling, so he was fine by me. Then the first words this guy spoke to me were: 'Hear me out here, but I have this theory.' I closed my sketchbook and sat up to listen.

He told me that he believed black people are from Mars, this bombshell dropped just before the mid-morning tea break. I spat my morning coffee across my notepad and laughed awkwardly, shocked by this curveball, but he looked at me with raised eyebrows and proceeded to try and convince me that the theory was more than just wild speculation. 'They f**ked it up, up there, you know.' He expanded on his statement by saying that 'they' had advanced way beyond our current civilisation, here on earth. 'Greed got the better of them and when they ruined Mars, they fled to Earth. It's obvious.' I told him he was entitled to believe what he wanted, but I thought he was completely deluded.

I continued to create new illustrations and flit between temporary jobs around Preston. Next up was ITV Pensions where I typed up box after box of deceased people's records into Excel spreadsheets. Then I was sent to Farmer's Books, a small business run by a local couple. Here I boxed customer orders including *The British Sausage Appreciation Society membership Book, 2007*. Then it was on to a company whose name eludes me, where they had me filing endless files in chronological order, where the old guys insisted that Classic Rock FM was never off the radio. Throughout all these jobs, I felt a burning, obsessive need to make the most of my creative skills, just like the one that had consumed me in 2004 while working at my dad's old workplace. I had to learn to find the hidden positives in these seemingly dull jobs, so I further subverted my warped sense of humour and got on with it.

Rich Taylor sent me the email address of a lady he'd worked with at Preston City Council. He suggested I contact her and send her a link to my website. Any kind of lead at this point had my heart racing with anticipation. I'd repeatedly refresh my email, just in case someone had contacted me, but there had been an error preventing its successful arrival. He said that the council usually had to use their in-house design department, but from time to time, they would turn to freelancers for some specialist work and he would put in a good word on my behalf. I hadn't considered that my local council might have a need for artwork. The email bounced back and it told me that the manager was away on maternity leave for the next few months.

A few days later her stand-in replacement, Debbie, came back to me and said she liked the look of my work. So I took her up on the offer of coming in and chatting about something she had in mind for me. The council's recycling team had been working hard to make recycling seem sexy to the large student population in the city and she wondered if I fancied putting something together to help their efforts. Unlike the first commission, which had a pre-determined budget on the table in front of me, for this one I was asked to quote for the

81 |

job. I didn't really have a clue. I hadn't negotiated anything financial since asking for a 90p advance on my paper-round to buy *Match* football magazine. In some areas, I still don't have a clue how to price a job. It is always a difficult thing to get a handle on. In the arts, licences, timings, duration of use, rights, territorial rights and all sorts of variables come into the equation. Thankfully, this job was simply for rolling out to the student properties and had no commercial usage to factor in, so I worked out how long it was likely to take me and quoted £900, estimating six days at the £150 day rate I figured I was worth.

For me at the time, £900 was an earthshaking sum of money, which they signed off without hesitation. To someone who had almost wept over the shattering of his last jar of peanut butter only weeks earlier, this changed everything. I was constantly terrified that the job would be pulled from under me at any moment. It seemed too perfect. It wasn't, and three weeks later, I sent Debbie a stupidly bright, clumsily composed student recycling calendar, covered in abstract representations of wheelie bins and recycling boxes. I did all the graphic design myself. You could tell; it looked like a village takeaway menu designed by Jackson Pollock. Nevertheless, they liked it because it was different and I had made almost a thousand pounds from my artwork, a sum that I would have had to work for over a month at Waterstones to earn.

With the job in the bag, I called into the council offices to find out the invoicing details and as I was about to leave, Debbie asked where I was currently working. I told her about the temporary job agency admin portal, into which I'd been swallowed into. She asked me if I'd be interested in working on the recycling team. I leaped on the opportunity. It wasn't illustration, but it sounded like a varied role, with a team of people and it paid better than the positions the agency was getting me. Most important of all was the fact that Preston's rent was cheap, so I could start to finance my business through the regular full-time work.

Taking on the council job was a smart move for me as an individual. Some people take the plunge and survive on scraps. Others take their time and like to fund their dream from roles in other jobs. It really depends on personalities and individual preference. I know some people who loathe the solitude that can come with working at home as an artist so much that they get a part-time job simply as a context for human interaction, even if they don't need it financially. Personally, I had no real plan yet, but I was never ready to throw myself in the deep end of full-time freelancing without some backing. Rash decisions would have been commonplace had I gone in too early and I have to be in a good headspace to make the right kind of considered calls.

I managed to pick up a few stray commissions within my department at the council, and would go and carry them out at the Stables. It all helped my saving plans and I now knew how to invoice without Google's help. My council role was 'recycling officer' and I got to drive a white transit van. I hadn't driven for four years since passing my test and it showed, but it meant I could cheekily call in at the stationers and pick up some supplies to drop off at the workshop without having to carry them from town.

The council offices were right by the Stables and if I came in early and skipped my lunch break, they let me go at 4pm, so I was on it by 4.15pm most weeknights and would stay until 11pm. I continued to spend most weekends in there, determined, developing my portfolio. The months passed by in this way and I started to grow more confident in my artistic ability while saving a chunk of my wage each week.

BUILDING THE NETWORK

Preston felt a lot smaller than it once had. I was settled into my routine of full-time work and matched the hours with creative time outside my weekday hours. Looking back, how I managed to dedicate all those evenings and weekends to illustration on top of my council job is beyond me. I was operating like a machine. Given my couple of tasters through the commissions I had taken on, the hunger to create things for a living was consuming me. I spent a lot of time looking through *The Guardian*, which was full of cool illustration. I longed so badly for that first major publication commission but I had not yet started to reveal my existence to the creative community.

The Guardian was positioned on a pedestal at university thanks to the paper's abundant use of good imagery and there were always several copies lying around the studio space that I would cut up and stick onto my partition wall. The idea of chasing WWE and Leeds United as dream clients was beyond comprehension at this point; I considered them gods in a mythical world, not of my earthbound Lancashire realm, since I had been fanatical about both sports from a young age. *The Guardian* was somehow more accessible and very much at the centre of my bulls-eye when I eventually reached a confidence level that allowed me to promote on a national scale to people who could pay me to draw.

One evening, I ran into Danny Allison, the guy I got along with from the year above me at university and went to see 'the Treehouse studio,' above a boutique in town, where he was now based. I was immediately envious. The place was nicely lit, all three tenants had desktop iMacs and pinned to their walls were cuttings of published jobs they had completed for clients I recognized. Even the music they played was fresh and trendy. It felt a bit like those school trips to museums where you get to talk to the drivers of steam engines or people who run stately homes, and ask them about their cool, unique jobs.

Danny brought me up to speed on his activity since university, showing me a bunch of magazines for which he'd recently been commissioned to illustrate and design. To see this first-hand, from a guy who had been at *my* university ,made it seem so much more attainable, even if envy now consumed me. To be honest, I was greener than frog shit, but more importantly, fiercely determined to try and make up some ground. It seemed that while I'd taken the scenic route, opting for the security of full time paid employment while I built up to a point where I felt ready for creative freelancing, he had gone in feet first, embracing the 'sink or swim' approach. He told me he was now very close to making a living entirely from illustration. His part time-job at Jessops photography shop was for ten hours a week and he was about to quit and go full-time freelance. I left with an open invitation to come by whenever I liked. I *needed* this in my life.

COMPETITIVE SPIRIT

Another memory of how horribly competitive I can be is fighting with a classmate because everyone was cheering my demise in the final of a knockout Wembley football game, simply because I was so easy to wind up in competition. I used to lose my temper in explosive fashion if I lost at any of the following:

- Competitive sport, mainly football and tennis. (I smashed a racket of my dad's when my 11-year-old brother turned me over at the age of 16).

- Board games.

- Video games: handsets have been broken and I reset my Sega Mastersystem by kicking it after losing one of three remaining lives on *Alex the Kidd*; back then you couldn't save your game and I cried intermittently for two days.

- Competitions: I spent weeks moaning when the older kid, who was runner up, was given the bigger and better Boglin toy when I, the winner, had been given the cheap, smaller one by the organizers of the local McDonald's colouring competition at six years old.

- Third party sports fixtures: I cried when Leeds United were relegated in 2004 and 2007 and when they lost in a standard league cup match against Leicester City, during the height of that particular obsession in 1999. I also cried on three separate occasions when Hulk Hogan was defeated or beaten up by The Undertaker, Earthquake and Sid Justice.

There are more horror stories of tantrums, but you get the idea. I've mellowed slightly in a couple of these areas. Now I started to see the beneficial side of this constant will to win at everything. Much like obsession, if you channelled it cleverly and effectively, it could be invaluable in business. Here I was, in Preston, knowing that right now, Danny Allison was quite simply a better illustrator than me, working for clients your parents have heard of and living entirely off the money. I thought about it every time I put on the big red rubber gloves for the council and fished through nappy filled bins. It chewed me up, but now I had a human benchmark to which I could aspire. I had ready access to his lair at the Treehouse Studio and planned to visit regularly.

- If your creative work feels like a chore, it's not the right style for you. Keep exploring.

- A website is crucial. It is your shop window and there are many cool, professional looking free portfolio sites until you can afford a full one.

- HTML website coding is a minefield, pay someone who understands it to do it for you or risk losing your mind.

- The Job Centre is a house of cards. It can be completely soul destroying, but also a holding pen for colourful characters.

- Despite the social stigma that is attached to it, being on the dole is nothing to be ashamed of and can be a necessary evil at times.

- Security guards are a law unto themselves.

- Upon landing your first commission and owning a website, you are invincible.

- The British Sausage Appreciation Society really exists.

- No matter how big a sum of money may sound, if it is fair, quote for it. Usually, it is not the personal money of the individual with the power to spend it, so they will not begrudge paying you properly unless you are taking the piss – there is always room for gentle negotiation.

- You have to put the hours in around your full- or part-time job, but beware of becoming trapped in full-time employment.

SAM PRICE: FREELANCE ART DIRECTOR, *TOP GEAR* MAGAZINE, *MATCH OF THE DAY* MAGAZINE, *Q* MAGAZINE, *BIG ISSUE* (ART DIRECTOR 2007-2011)

'Every magazine is a different realm. I've been at Q, Kerrang, and FourFourTwo recently. I worked at one magazine and it was kicking off in the office. I walked over to show a page to the guy I was working for. 'How's this looking?' He takes the page off me, screws it up and throws it back at me. He starts screaming and shouting. It had nothing to do with me but he's in my face. I'm there going… I mean I'm not even bothered, you can't engage with someone when they're just totally aggressive, you know what I mean? It was something to do with press shots and it was between NME and the place I'm at and some Stone Roses pictures were printed in NME but not released to these guys.

The office has gone painfully quiet and the young guy next to me looks worried. The permanent staff have all looked at me with a collective expression of, 'What are you doing?!' I was like, 'I'm just doing my job. What?' And it's like – 'Nice one there.' They've just laughed it off but it's just how he runs it. They know him from experience and just pussyfoot around him. I've gone in to query one headline and he's just lost it. There's a lot of that. A lot of editors marshall by fear. I'll move something on a page by maybe 3mm and everyone is huffing and puffing, 'You can't do that!' And you better not show it to the editor. Everywhere has their own little emperor that you have to be accepted by.

The thing is, I'm a grown man. People try it on with a 17-year-old boy, but I'm a man, taking this from a 55-year-old man, who is 5'8. You're not going to say this to me in a pub. But that's the politics of a workplace I guess. It is just power and it's quite interesting when you see that. If you'd passed on a bad design, then you bite the bullet and get the job done, but there was nothing there and he's just like, 'gggrrrrooouuuaaarrrgghhh!!!!' He just had that anger and had to let it out. I just had to laugh. I'd been there a week and the rest of the team just grin. He didn't turn up the next day, maybe the stress. It's an eye-opener seeing the politics of it all.'

CHAPTER 6. STARTING AT THE BOTTOM

Oyston Mill was an old mill building down near Preston docks that had a range of different sized spaces available. We were quoted a price that was only a little more than the rates at the Stables. Several people with whom we shared decided to leave, so Rich Taylor, Danny Allison and two other friends moved into Oyston Mill. To work from home again at this point would have been career suicide.

I couldn't stop thinking about how cool Danny's position as a full-time freelancer must be, illustrating all week, every week. So I made a bold plan. My website was live. I was registered with HMRC. My confidence was growing and I felt ready to lay down some targets and stick to them. If I could save enough money to live on for three months, I could justify quitting my job at the council. It was risky; my peanut butter heartbreak had underlined that, but recent progress since signing on benefits had taught me that if you don't take risks, you don't go anywhere. If the money ran out and I didn't make any through freelancing, so be it, I would find the next job to pay my bills or I would reacquaint myself with the Job Centre. I had nothing to lose. The main thing was that I maximized the time on my hands by planting seeds in the short term, without worrying what came next.

I talked to my bosses at the council and they were very supportive of my move and said to let them know if I ever needed work. I handed in my notice and have to admit, I felt sad. I had made some close friends and had a wonderful time in that job. I just couldn't ignore the burning desire to be an illustrator any longer and I was ready to take the plunge, in good time to meet my original deadline of Euro 2008, which England had failed to reach.

FULL-TIME FREELANCE?

Oyston Mill was huge and freezing in the winter and the internet seemed to be our only link to the present day. The cold would seep up through the thick concrete floors, beneath our feet. My parents didn't drive, so they never saw any of these ropey studios when they came to visit. If they had, it would have kept them awake at night imagining their firstborn scratching around in the sub-zero shadow dens, like some sort of ghost. The room was massive, so we each had effectively a full office worth of space, divided only by partition walls that stood about four feet high, plus a communal drinks and eating area, with a second-hand sofa. I had my own little bookshelf with my illustration compendiums that I had bought with my Waterstones staff discount towards the end of my time in the job.

Our room in Oyston Mill had a weird little corner booth that had a dried out, faded pile of bodybuilding magazines in a carrier bag, most likely left by the previous occupants, and when we tried to rip down the structure, some solid iron weightlifting bars fell through the roof, missing Rich's head by millimetres. We always felt close to death in that place.

I was now living in an end-of-terrace house with my two previous housemates, which was a five-minute walk down the road from the mill. The house was as cold as the studio with a bonus chronic damp problem. The single glazing felt like the windows were made of clingfilm and the heating did whatever it wanted to do. During the summer, we were infested with flying ants. Some friends had started to take out mortgages, the idea of which felt as far away from my life as Botox™ and paparazzi, but I had a lot to gain over the next 12 weeks and that was all I truly cared about.

The first thing I noticed about full-time freelancing was the immense pressure - this giant invisible egg timer containing not sand, but my three month's living costs slowly spiralling downwards. The fact that I held my future partially in my own hands was exciting and nerve-wracking.

I promised myself that I would not waste the opportunity so I arrived at 7am on my first day. Music on. Kettle on. Then what? It was a strange moment, looking out of the window, over the Preston docks on a grey, dry morning in winter, plumes of my breath rolling up like smoke. I ignored any phone calls that were not work-related and banned myself from Facebook, Leeds United and wrestling news until my lunch breaks each day. Lunch was a sandwich made up from the cheapest food I could manage to live on for a week, usually costing around £8. If I bought couscous, I was unstoppable.

Before approaching any clients, I wanted to spend a solid fortnight fine-tuning my portfolio, making sure it was as good as it could possibly be, so I set about a piece I had started, on the front of the scavenged monitor from the Stables, which had somehow made it to studio number two. I had painted the front of the glass screen with acrylic paint and was in the process of persevering with my collage style, gluing on one of my anatomy photocopy bodies. It had no direction and the style was nothing short of insane, like a picture version of a serial killer's journal.

Danny came in about 10am and immediately he was on the phone, cup of tea in hand, chatting to a real client about a real commission. I listened and spied over the partition wall, a total voyeur, creatively aroused by the prospect of ever taking such a raunchy phone call. We talked complete nonsense all day and took turns making pots of tea. I couldn't have been happier. Despite the pressure to make things happen sooner rather than later, I had all day, every day at my disposal and my money would last for three months if I used it wisely.

Danny came around to my part of the studio in the afternoon, which I had started to call 'the squared circle' on my email footers. This was after the nickname for a professional wrestling ring that the commentators threw around on the WWE shows.

'Can I be honest with you?' he asked. 'Yeah, of course.' I knew what was coming, I just hadn't admitted it to myself yet. 'I say what I think and some people think I'm a dick for it, but I don't really care. If you take this the wrong way, then that's up to you, but I'm going to say it anyway.' I felt I was about to be given the school corridor telling-off treatment.

He continued: 'I'm not sure what you are doing on that monitor, but there are a thousand better collage artists out there. Your drawing is second to none and I never did understand why you never used it more in your work at uni. So I think you should lead with that. This style isn't working, that looks shit. What do you reckon?'

I wasn't sure what to say, but I had been cornered, forced to face the truth. I had that sinking feeling that comes with knowing you will have to start everything again, but I had no excuses. In truth, I had never really enjoyed the process of this half-baked style, only the occasional finished product, but you tend to rush into deciding on your 'style' and shy away from taking the time to experiment and find out what truly works for you.

The weeks would be long; putting together a whole new folder, but with the lads I had with me in this studio, it was plain to see that I could rely on honest criticism and a lot of fun. I couldn't tell you when I had stopped drawing. From the age of about four I had loved to draw. Over years, I had become pretty good at it, yet somewhere along the way, I had become distracted with other, trendier styles of image-making.

I saw so much gorgeous full colour illustration in *The Guardian* and other benchmark publications, that I had placed unnecessary pressure on myself to perfect a style closer to the current trends. After Danny's honest lashing, I decided... You have to do what you love and *set* the trend. Trends are nothing but creative masturbation and they change constantly. If you allow them to, they'll drop you without warning and then you're stuffed. So I endeavoured to create a punchy style with character and soul, then trust that it would have a place, no matter what was flavour of the month.

The style I had in mind seemed brilliant, but my draftsmanship and technical skills were limited, so I had grown frustrated.

I bought myself a pen, a pot of ink, a load of fine line pens and a range of papers. Something clicked almost instantly. The drawing came so naturally to me that I had my first piece finished in an hour or so. By the end of the second day in Oyston Mill, I had turned around four illustrations with black ink on paper. I would create a separate layer of colour, scan it into the computer and combine the two. The style looked original, consistent and had a distinct life to it that the heavy, painterly collages were seriously lacking.

The freedom to draw whatever I wanted, afforded by this breakthrough, set me off on a fortnight of 14-plus hour work benders, from 7am until midnight, with only an hour to go home and eat my tea. I couldn't stop. Danny and I would sit there late into the evenings, sometimes illuminated only by the halogen heater light or streetlight outside the window. His company kept me going when I flagged, his brutal honesty was a crucial factor in speeding up my stylistic progression. Seeing a project through to its conclusion was a huge thrill and I was addicted.

The cut off from the outside world (aside from the occasional visit to say hello to the council ex-colleagues) sent me down a rabbit hole of madness. I was embarking upon a dream job odyssey with no external policing whatsoever. Danny was hilarious and knew no behaviour boundaries. The conversations we had in that room took on their own life and they started to make Rich cry with laughter. They also started to influence my work in a big way. Some of that early work is still in my portfolio.

I drew a massive penguin towering over a terrorist and wrote the words, 'Silly F**king Humans' largely down frustrations about my race. Danny designed a popular t-shirt, depicting Christ the Redeemer dropping bombs, which read 'Religion is Dangerous.' That earned him both popularity and a Catholic backlash, asking him to remove the piece from his website. One day, he told Leona, his girlfriend, that he was going to take her parents out with them to feed the ducks, grabbed a loaf of bread and drove up to Beacon Fell. He screeched the car to a halt in the road when he saw what he was really after. Getting out and dropping to one knee, Danny bagged up a pheasant that had been run over by a car. Leona and her parents looked on aghast. He said he was sick of over-reliance on stock images as he handed the carrier bag containing the bird to her silenced dad in the back seat, clambered back in the driver's seat and photographed his bounty the next day in the studio, before disposing of it. He used the images to create an artwork referencing the battery farming of chickens.

That year, I sent out a rather dark-natured Christmas card indiscriminately to prospective clients in an effort to stand out from the crowd, featuring elves engaging in violent combat with hooded villains in the street. Among the oddities, I managed to create some pretty cool conceptual illustrations that I could send to magazines and newspapers. The time had come to stop hiding behind my email and pick up the phone.

KEN GARLAND, BRITISH GRAPHIC DESIGNER AND AUTHOR OF *THE FIRST THINGS FIRST MANIFESTO*

'If you have to fight, you feel better about results, provided you win. But I have a type of person in mind and that's the gentle, shy person who is talented but cannot shout too well. Unless the talent in those people is nurtured, it will not see the light of day, so I don't think it is only the pushy person who should be respected here. It's tougher than it used to be, but will the ones who really want to be successful and press for it win the day? No! It's not that simple! The sensitive people need recognition and they need tutors who respond to the incipient talent and ensure that kind of person receives the training they need. I've seen quieter colleagues flourish with the right support.'

HI, MY NAME IS

After two weeks of 14-hour marathons, my portfolio was about 20 images strong and the old style was completely obsolete. The cold in both my house and Oyston Mill had become unbearable. Every visit to the toilet, which was at the end of the corridor, was a near-death experience. We bought a 99p football from the garage shop over the road and booted it around the spacious corridor, which was almost as big as a five-a-side pitch. That kept us warm. I was putting two working week's worth of time into every week. If I had to return to employment, I couldn't face the guilt that would follow if that was down to a lack of effort on my part.

A couple of us split the cost of a copy of *The Artists and Writers Yearbook* using my staff discount from Waterstones. That would be my starting point. I was about to get going but the thought of cold calling anyone made me feel a little nauseous. It was bad enough calling mothers who wanted bigger wheelie-bins, let alone art directors in London, who held all the cards, but what alternative did I have? I had built them up as myths and legends in my mind.

I started a spreadsheet database and typed up every one of the publications from the book, listing all their contact details. For the next three weeks, I ploughed through it in alphabetical order. Every conversation felt awkward and I stuttered a lot. As a northerner, I found it intimidating that all these clients had southern accents, which is, of course, outrageously silly, but I had spent my whole 25 years in the north of England, save for a few family trips to London as a kid, so they somehow seemed more elegant and I imagined they were all more worldly than me. It made me painfully aware of my missing letters and words in a Yorkshire accent. That didn't help matters.

'Oh... Hi! My name is Ben Tallon, I'm a-'

'Sorry, I missed that, can you say it again?'

'Yeah, sorry, my name is B...B...B...Ben Tallon... I'm a freelance illustrator, would you mind if I sent you over s...s... some of my work?'

'Yeah no worries, please do, if you could send it to this email.'

I had heart palpitations every time I got off the phone and

had to make a cup of tea every three or four calls to swerve some sort of emotional collapse. The calls would go one of three ways:

'Great, yes, send your website link to this address and we'll keep you on file.'

'We don't use illustration but send the samples anyway and you never know.'

'We only use photography, goodbye.'

Every now and again, someone would be friendly and chat to me, maybe even pass my details to another magazine title in the building if they were extra nice. Once in a while, someone would ask where I found their contact details, sounding as if I'd purloined the records from MI5. The nice responses were worth waiting for. You'd get the occasional northerner who would ask where I was from. I made a separate little spreadsheet for anyone who had stayed on the line for more than ten seconds. I figured I could focus on them and take more care to tailor my approach to their needs. In other words, the value of targeted and carefully focused promotion had only just occurred to me.

I often mistook efficiency for rudeness, which is easy to do when you're made of eggshell in your early days. The truth is: art directors, like every person in the arts, are horrendously busy, receiving many identical phone calls and emails each day. It is their job to work with creative professionals, but if they spent all day on the phone, they would get nothing done, so eventually, I learned that they were just doing what they had to do, like me.

Danny, in his own words is 'a modern day gypsy'. He shared all these canny little tricks and tips with me. On one occasion, he called a company's switchboard in London and said he urgently needed to speak with the art director of a certain magazine. When the receptionist asked to what the call was in relation, (the question that will determine whether the art director accepts or declines the call) he said: 'Oh, I'm supposed to be sending them an illustration and I've had some technical difficulties.' In such a scenario, the receptionist then panics and either hands you the details or puts you straight through as urgent. Technically, he isn't lying about needing to send an illustration and then he is through to his target.

I made it to the listings under G.

G for *The Guardian*. This national newspaper used upwards of 30 illustrations in some weekend editions. I had to stand a chance if I remained persistent, didn't I? The listing in the book informed me that the design director was Roger Browning. Rogers are friendly, aren't they? I called the number and got the switchboard. They asked me to hold the line. Without so much as a dialing tone, there was a click and the static was replaced by many bustling voices and the hum of phones ringing. 'Hello, Roger Browning...' I swallowed the panic breath rising in my throat and gave him the mantra, voice wavering, telling him my name, my job and courteously asked if he had a minute to chat. 'No I'm afraid I don't have a minute, goodbye.' The harsh click of termination ringing in my ears, then dead-tone, terminal beep. Rejection. Searing emotional pain. Returning to the cold silence of Oyston Mill, I slowly put my phone on the desk and watched my spirit create a layer of condensation on the window, before escaping through the single pane of glass, belly flopping gracelessly into the Preston docks and drowning.

♦ ROGER BROWNING: DESIGN DIRECTOR, *THE GUARDIAN*, 1995-2013

'I think timing is something creatives need to be aware of. If you are approaching someone at a newspaper, the best time to call us is in the morning. That's when we're perhaps not as busy. If you call up at 5 in the afternoon, we're bound to be snowed under. Especially if we're working on the next day's issue. If you call on a Thursday, some art directors are right on deadline for four sections of the weekend edition of the paper. There are times when you cannot humanly reply. If I get it early, when I'm not busy I will reply. I try to reply to everyone.'

My moment with Roger Browning was essential and ruthlessly necessary, but for a short minute or so, I was livid, offended and all shaken up. *Toughen up.* If the pleasant and routine phone calls had built my confidence brick by brick, the heartbreak I felt when Roger put down the phone on me didn't do a demolition job, but laid Roman columns. Welcome to the business world, leave your feelings at the door. I gave myself a day off from phone calls and buried myself in some drawing.

A mere 48 hours later, relationship break-up style, I got fired up and stopped sulking. It was the only way forward. Shaking, partly from the cold and partly from nerves, I dialled *The Guardian* again, defiant. They put me through to Roger and he answered quickly once again. I took a deep breath and was stunned to be greeted by a friendly, bubbly Kiwi voice. He asked me when I was going to come and see him. This caught me completely off guard and we pencilled in a date, agreeing to go for coffee in Farringdon, where *The Guardian* offices were based at that time. I got off the phone and Danny gave me some sort of skater hand gesture, which I assumed was congratulatory, the wiggle of his little finger and thumb being driven home by a huge, 'Yeeaaaahhh!!!!!' and all of a sudden, I was a teenager who had been shown interest by a pretty girl, actually blushing and grinning widely. I had to put the kettle on.

ARE YOU AVAILABLE?

The second call to Roger triggered the buses theory and three opportunities came along at once. Each day I would call many people and email them the link to my website. I would call them back a couple of days later to get some feedback, a tip given to me by Danny. He said that way, they would hear from me three times and would be far likelier to take notice than if I had simply emailed once and waited. They might even remember me. In the evenings, I would go about creating new pieces, to give me more reasons to pester them and develop a stronger portfolio.

In my indiscriminate, A-Z, blanket-style way of approaching potential clients, I had sent out my edgier illustrations to everyone in *The Artists and Writers Yearbook*. Of course, I loved my own work, but my distinct style was not right for everyone's needs. I sent the illustration of hooded youths beating up an elf to *Practical Pregnancy Magazine* and *Boots' Parenting Club Magazine*. I really didn't think about the client's readership at all and while the recipients were all polite and complimentary, they were shell-shocked by my bizarre subject matter. The distinctive urban style was off, even if I had drawn a baby or a nappy. I was told never to contact *Dogs Today* again, after approaching them three times in three days, simply because I loved dogs and believed they would give me my first published job. Owning a Staffordshire bull terrier, it would seem, is not a licence to harass dog publications.

When Saturday Comes (WSC) is a satirical football magazine that serves a more 'indie audience' than its glossy competitor, *FourFourTwo* magazine. I discovered that it uses illustration when I stumbled across an archive of the magazine in the journal section of my university library and placed WSC alongside *The Guardian* at the peak of my desired client list. Since being issued the figurative restraining order by *Dogs Today*, I started to think that I should perhaps consider more carefully which publications my work would suit and that it could be a good idea to lead with subjects that I knew something about. Exhibiting this knowledge creatively might endear me to these hand-picked clients and make up some of the deficit I suffered given the absence of commissioned work in my portfolio. I put together a conceptual illustration and sent it to WSC's art director. He came back to me quite quickly, saying he thought the style was cool and suited WSC's content. He would keep me in mind for future issues.

This was becoming a frequent response to my approaches and, admittedly, I began to doubt its validity. The long days on the phone, contacting magazines, are trying. When you send out more than 100 emails in a week and only four people acknowledge you, it hurts and it's easy to fall into a confidence black hole. I didn't see it getting any better, but the breakthrough with Roger at *The Guardian* and now *WSC* had given me a real boost.

A year-and-a-half after our trip to London for the New Blood exhibition, I would be heading back to the capital to see Roger Browning, Design Director of *The Guardian*. I thought it would be foolish not to try to schedule some more portfolio meetings since I would be spending the money on a return ticket anyway. So I now needed to be even more robust, asking for ten minutes of potential clients' time. To my surprise, only one or two said 'no' and that was down to being too busy. So I booked in about eight or nine meetings. Now all I had to do was find somewhere to stay. I scoured the hostel booking websites, since hotels were way out of my price bracket and my money was slowly dissipating. In the end, I liked the look of a place in Brixton, called 'The Hootenanny'. It had a cool building exterior, Brixton featured in one of The Clash's more famous tracks, and it cost only £11 a night.

In the midst of scheduling all these meetings, I had focused only on my trip, assuming that there would be no work to worry about. Then one morning as I stood chatting to Rich and Danny, my phone started to ring and displayed a London number. I nearly shit my pants. I looked up at Danny with a look of shock, panic, hope and fear all at once and said, 'It's a London number, you think it could be...?' Danny started to laugh and shouted, 'Well answer it then, you dickhead, or you'll never know!' So I accepted the call. It was the art director from WSC and he wanted to know if I was available to create an illustration for the next issue. I slipped into some kind of trance. Danny's grinning face, peeping over the partition wall, watching me fall apart, is all I remember.

My mind came back into the room with a kind of 'whooooosh' noise as the phone call ended. I had to call him back after a cup of tea to find out the fee for the job and have him run over the details a second time. I didn't remember anything from our conversation. I had fantasized about this moment for two years and when it happens, you just pull a stupid face and have a tiny emotional breakdown in full view of everyone.

The stress of the subsequent 24 hours will, one day, manifest itself in baldness or premature greying. I had to get a rough sketch over to WSC by the end of the day and the final artwork, inclusive of amendments, by the close of play (5pm) the following day. They paid me £150 for the artwork and the article was a single page opinion piece about Ian Wright's new role, presenting the remake of 1990s colossal Saturday evening TV show, *Gladiators*. The pressure I imposed on myself was gargantuan. I worked up a satisfactory pencil sketch, put the kettle on and started to shake.

Milestones of this magnitude don't allow you time to think about or plan your reaction. It wasn't just my first commission in a major publication. Hell, it was football, but it was also Ian Wright, a legend of the game. The last time I had held anything to do with Ian Wright in my hands, I was caught stealing his Corinthian football action figurine, earning me a ban from all UK Woolworths stores; my one foray into crime at 12 years old.

Now here I was drawing him for money. I sat there with a work-in-progress at 8pm, staring blankly at the screen. Danny came round to check on me and said he was going home and I was coming with him to watch a film. I protested and he said that if I stayed now, in this frayed state of mind,

I would mess it all up, trust him, he'd been there too often. No good can come of being in this mindset. I reluctantly followed him and I thought of nothing but the job all night. I slept for a broken three hours and returned at 6.30am the next day, with big grey bags under my eyes. It turned out to be a waste of good energy. With a fresh eye, it was easy to see that the illustration was the strongest thing I had done so far and WSC loved it, but you're flirting with complacency when stress is absent, so the insomnia was inevitable. I had performed on 'the big stage' and felt pretty good about it.

I wrote my first proper invoice, logo header and everything, sent it with a few too many thanks and packed for London, safe in the knowledge I was a professional, proper, published illustrator.

 VICTORIA PEARCE: FORMER FASHION AND PHOTOGRAPHY AGENT, CURRENT AGENT AT ILLUSTRATION LTD

'My love of the illustration side of things grew. I fell in love with the art of where the human hand had been – the skill involved and how natural that is. My great grandfather was a member of C R Ashby's Guild of Handicrafts so I had been brought up with an appreciation of hand skills and making tradition. My father was a photographer, my sister is a shoemaker and my husband is a jeweller.

Eve Stoner and I saw the business going in different directions. We set up Fashion-Art.com to sell prints and expanded the business. Some of our photographers felt

that it couldn't work if were representing both illustrators and photographers. Three of our most established photographers parted company with us and suddenly it felt like we were driving this juggernaut that was out of control and we put the business into administration which was heartbreaking at the time, as we had been successful and were well respected in the creative community.

David Downton had come on board and after Pearce-Stoner Associates, he introduced me to Harry Lyon-Smith who had been running Illustration Ltd for over 20 years. David felt I could bring something to their business and Harry offered me a job as an agent. I was very happy to accept, David had taken on the role of my fairy godfather and here was an absolute gift horse. Jacqueline came with me from Pearce-Stoner Associates. I was very sad to leave behind my own agency, but excited to join a specialized agency with fantastic talent, working in new areas such as children's books, packaging and much more.'

MEETING CLIENTS

I arrived at the Hootenanny bar and hostel in Brixton, south east London, clutching two massive bags containing my week's worth of clothes, my laptop and portfolio. It dawned on me that this was my first lone trip to the capital. It could all go wrong. I was clutching a copy of *WSC* from the WHSmith next to Brixton tube station. I shoved it straight in the face of the first person that made eye contact with me after check in. I couldn't have been happier to see my work adorning the page of a real life, nationally circulated magazine. The hostel part of The Hootenanny was directly above the bar, which hosted live reggae, ska, blues and punk music. It was full of people from all over the world and handily located, even if the kitchen was grotty and noisy around the clock. Frankly, I didn't care, I was now a published illustrator, therefore invincible.

My week comprised staring at tube maps, sweating and finding myself lost en route to meetings in the day, wearing a pair of smart trousers, a shirt and black shoes. I probably overdressed, given my profession, but nobody knew who I was, so I wanted to look like I could be trusted to work for their publication. I looked like a clueless tourist, but at least I was presentable. My dorm slept 10 people and was cheap, but also a pit of foul odours and untidiness. I didn't care, I was a published illustrator.

I visited the *Big Issue* where I met Sam Price, the art director, and Jim Ladbury, the magazine's designer. I had an inroad through Danny Allison who had been doing artwork for them for a couple of years. Our styles are quite different so he selflessly introduced me to Sam over email. A personal recommendation in the creative world is immensely valuable. The first clients you meet are larger-than-life and I was always slightly fearful of a low trouser fly or walking dog mess onto the reception carpets. Threats were everywhere. Sam was a Liverpool fan and we talked mainly football before quickly leafing through my portfolio together.

The designer at the *Big Issue* asked me where I was staying. Upon mention of my Hootenanny accommodation, his jaw dropped. He lived a stone's throw away, but had no knowledge of its secret hostel-by-night alter ego. It turns out the authorities were rumoured to have turned a blind eye to the place. He said it 'kicked off' there, regularly. The place was a hangout for 'characters' and, in the past, if you wanted to pursue your chosen vice, or anything else, it was the heart of that world in Brixton. These days, it was said to be a little safer, but the idea of staying there blew his mind.

I laughed and shrugged my shoulders. After all, I was now a published illustrator, therefore not at risk from knives, shooters, drugs, gangs or any other assorted irritations. That being said, on the third day, at tea time, I sat struggling to wind the noodles in my Thai evening meal as three blokes with stockings over their heads burst in and smashed up the fruit machine, taking all the money. It remains the only time I've seen a heist in real life, if you can call it that. But I thought about the fact I was now a full-time illustrator with work in all 'good newsagents', wiped my mouth and cast my eye unflinchingly over the dessert menu.

Aside from the *Big Issue*, no meetings lasted longer than five minutes. The art directors all seemed to like my work and they gained a feel for my style in one or two flicks through my portfolio. This was a good thing. My drawing-led work had changed everything and the work now packed (previously lacked) personality. The enjoyment had become evident in each piece and it showed.

Heading north east to Farringdon, I was extremely nervous about entering *The Guardian* HQ. The reception was adorned with all kinds of hipness; brightly coloured type printed on the walls, various copies of the paper left for visitors to read while they sat on cool chairs designed to support posture (or something like that). Even the security gates were electric and studded with blue lights. I felt like an invader, a country boy from the Northern Time Continuum, attempting to hide under a cheap shirt and badly ironed trousers, but Roger came down to fetch me and instantly put me at ease. For a design director who must have been horrendously busy at all times, he was very relaxed and friendly.

We made our way to a café across the road where he bought me coffee. We sat there and chatted for 20 minutes about music and art. He told me about coming to live in London from New Zealand and said *The Guardian* was a cool place to work. He particularly liked a boxing poster I had mocked up, featuring Barack Obama and Hilary Clinton, which read 'The race v sex challenge,' with a strapline: 'Forget policies, he's black and she's a woman!' He liked the political angle I had taken and said its simplicity was endearing. He asked if I could work fast and I told him that my style was quick to execute. Newspapers, he told me, are ruthless, given their daily turnaround. I told him about my love of many sports and he said that this sporting knowledge was an attractive trait because *The Guardian Sport*, in particular, could throw up nightmarishly tight deadlines allowing no time to educate the freelancer on subject matter. I would most likely need to wait until the summer before any opportunities would become available, but was advised to keep sending over new work and remind Roger I existed from time to time.

I wrapped up my week's meetings and felt like things were starting to come together. I got very drunk that weekend, so drunk that I understood six new languages including Polish, Spanish, Greek and Welsh. By 4am on Sunday morning, four of us were caught dragging a double mattress up the stairs, knocking vases off window ledges and waking up other guests, giggling. The Hootenanny had double-booked our beds and there were now strangers sleeping in them and drunk people swaying in the halls, causing havoc. We got the mattress into a room that was being decorated and managed to fit all four of us on the bed. They kicked us out in the morning and I made my way back to Preston with my capital hangover. I didn't care, I was a published illustrator and I had just met the design director of *The Guardian*.

- Many financial and lifestyle risks are required to make serious progress in the freelance world.

- Mortgages can feel like alien concepts to a new freelancer; light years away and mythical. Ignore them and focus on being happy, riches will come with success, and success is a by-product of enjoying your creativity.

- Pressure can be overwhelming during the first stages of the transition to self-employment, but using it positively helps keep complacency at bay.

- Facebook is the enemy and will gobble your time if you allow it to. Make it a lunchtime treat and save it for after work. Nothing that cannot wait is ever happening on social media.

- Listen to criticism. If you have someone in your world willing provide honest feedback, take it all on board and act on it. They are invaluable people to have, not the enemy. An iron chin is a part of the freelance starter pack and taking offence is futile.

- Lead with your stylistic strengths and the rest will come with practice

- Do not be afraid to start again if you have a creative revelation, whether on an individual piece or entire portfolio.

- Trends are discernible in the arts, but creative output with personality and individualism is timeless. Make the trends follow you.

- Insular and quirky projects will connect with many because of originality.

- You have to start somewhere. Get stuck in. Your portfolio can always be better. It will never be perfect, so pick up the phone, email and visit people. Let your market know you exist.

- Persevere and pester. Some clients will tell you to piss off, others will respond to your hustling. Not everyone will like your work. If you want to make an omelette, you have to break some eggs.

- Fine-tune your focus. If your work is topical or stylized, do not waste time sending drawings of street attacks on elves to *Practical Pregnancy.*

- Efficiency is not rudeness. Clients are busy people, bear with them, but be robust in your approach. 'No' is not an acceptable answer, but you might have to get through many rejections to find your openings.

- Rejection is tough, but for every 20 knock-backs, there's a door slightly ajar for you to force open.

- Hostels are great fun and a cheap way of staying in London, if you can hack the hygiene and noise flaws. Use them and mingle.

- Clients are superheroes when you're starting out, but are people like you; respect them but do not fear them.

- Getting your first published commission is a life-affirming buzz. Do whatever it takes to get it and run with it.

CHAPTER 7. BACK TO REALITY

Several commissions for *WSC* and meeting *The Guardian*, *The Big Issue* and *The Times* had left me dizzy. I made around £450 over three months with *WSC* and suggested we could do a deal which would guarantee me a regular slot. It didn't happen, on the basis that some months there was no way they could be certain there would be an article that required my style of illustration, but at least it underlined my desire to work for them.

My small town-perfected ability to talk to most people quite easily was becoming something of a magic wand, with some sterling belief under my belt. A touch paper had been lit after I rounded off that first job and I was craving more. I continued to produce new portfolio work and explore markets that used, or could potentially use, illustration. My database grew by the day and I continued to have a lot of fun in Oyston Mill. If I found a tattered newspaper supplement magazine on the train, I'd log the contact details on my phone and put them in my database back at the mill. Any time to kill was now murdered in WHSmiths where I hurriedly plundered as many contact details from their shelves as I could before they started asking questions.

I speculatively mocked up illustrations for articles in *The Guardian* and put them in context on the page, before sending them to Roger. Nobody had told me any of this stuff, but as my initiative was given more of a workout, I started to push the envelope to rise above others who might be relying on less robust methods of self-promotion. Roger said my work was getting better and reiterated that he'd try find an article for me to illustrate in the summer. I felt light-headed at the thought of any work for *The Guardian*, even a tiny spot illustration tucked away, out of sight, made me all jelly-legged. I bought the paper quite often, which had become a guilty pleasure, drooling over the cover illustration on the 'weekend' magazine. At 14, it was *FHM*'s '100 sexiest' that I'd smuggle past my mate's mum. Now it was the broadsheets.

My money started to run thin around the four-month mark. The earnings from *WSC* had stretched my full-time illustration career to four months, one better than the initial goal, but not enough to live off. I had kept in contact with my friends and former colleagues at Preston City Council and when I mentioned that I would soon have to consider a part-time work position until I could earn a full-time living, they said there was a chance of two days-a-week back in my old role, if I wanted it. The manager was still away on maternity leave and some of my old colleagues had been helping in other departments, so it may help them out to have someone driving the vans and providing a bit of extra manpower around the place. This was perfect.

I refused to see my return to employment in a negative light. I had made some huge steps forward, worked incredibly hard and secured my first client who had returned with two more commissions. Meeting others in person, who all seemed genuinely keen, meant I was in a good place. The trip to London had opened my eyes. Given how easy it would be to rely on digital dependence, getting lazy and sitting in my office, relying on emails and social media to promote my work was a real threat. But Roger's unforeseen invitation to come and see *The Guardian* had left me no choice but to go and meet some humans, and it was to be a pivotal invitation.

As a creative professional of any kind, you are essentially a salesman and your product is something created from nothing for use in visual media. You can either create the product and then find a market, or find a market to commission you to create the product. Either way, asking someone to pay you to do that in person was far likelier to bear fruit than doing it over email. They could see you were real, not just another digital leech, clinging to the inside wall of their email inbox, suckling on their precious time. They had the chance to get to know and like you (hopefully), and most importantly, making the effort to drag yourself out of the office, in order to see them, would show dedication. There are a number of game-changing traits that cannot be conveyed in an email or on social media:

- Body language
- Humour
- Personality
- Individuality
- Passion

I was like a child in an adventure park in London, jumping on underground trains, visiting all kinds of galleries and having pints of Guinness at lunchtime, something I hadn't enjoyed since my student years had ended. In the bigger companies, they give you visitor passes with the company logo on them and I tried to steal the one from *The Guardian*, just in case my creative flirtation with them never progressed to the desired fling; but they asked me for it back as I crept past reception and, to be fair, I wouldn't be helping my chances by running off with it.

Now, all I was lacking was money and here was a timely offer of re-employment, two days-a-week, in a job with which I was comfortable, with people I liked. The cherry on the cake came when the department manager told me he was aware that I had an illustration career to consider now and that I could switch my days at short notice, if a job came in. He instantly became the latest in a line of heroes.

PART-TIME BENEFITS

Tuesdays and Thursdays at the council had multiple benefits. They provided me with a measure of reality to offset the psychedelia going on at the studio. The job got me outdoors for just the right amount of time and the summer was a decent one. It paid me the crucial money that enabled me to continue spending the rest of my week promoting my artwork and my council colleagues showed genuine interest in my progress.

If there was any danger of getting carried away with my first achievements as an illustrator, these were well and truly put in perspective by the general public and bins. The big red rubber gloves were back on and the dirty nappies I avoided for four months were reintroduced into my working life.

How it worked was: a pissed off person would phone the council who would put them through to my 'litter and recycling department', complaining about the family wheelie bin overflowing. I'd be deployed in a luminous high-visibility jacket, with oversized steel toe cap boots, for the person to peck my head, while the nappies burst, revealing stomach-turning contents not fit for a bluebottle. I'd occasionally grant them a bigger bin, but most times, it was full of recyclables so I would reach the safety of the phone back at the offices, then call up and tell the family member that until they recycled their papers, cards, plastics, glasses and food waste properly, the family would not be getting the requested upgrade. Then I'd hold the phone a foot from my ear while I did some sketching or some council paperwork, cartoon style, shouting mouth coming out the phone and barking at me. After another 10 minutes of profanity from the rejected citizen, I'd put the phone back to my ear and pencil in another visit for the following week to see if the family had bucked up their ideas, then run back to the safety of Oyston Mill and my sketchbooks.

Roger Browning called during my council lunch break one Tuesday. When you're new to the game, your brain instantly defaults to preparation for the disappointment scenario to be played out in the face of an opportunity. It takes years to start believing something good *could* actually come your way, even when it's got you by the balls screaming in your face. Roger was most likely just checking in to see how I was doing. I was wrong and he asked if I was available to do a job for *The Guardian*. Job for *The Guardian*. *Job for The ACTUAL Guardian*. His last four words echoed around my brain like a gunshot in a vacuum. Off I went again, into my trance, whizzing through time and space. Ben Tallon's body was anchored to the second floor of the city council offices on Argyle Road, Preston, but his mind had shattered into hundreds of shards, all over the floor and were spinning across far away universes and alternate dimensions.

I'd predicted a low-risk, spot illustration; instead, Roger wanted me to create the artwork for the front cover of that Friday's *Guardian Film and Music* pull-out section of the newspaper. A schizophrenic seesaw of unbridled hysteria and perfect silence was at play in my head and I sat in the staircase area for five minutes running my hands through my hair, breaking into a cold sweat.

I eventually ran into the council office and shouted a string of consonants that nobody understood. On the second attempt, I told them the good news and felt like the king of the world. It paid £360, which was one hell of a rate compared to my part-time earnings. I started to see there were not only tangible dreams for the taking, but good money to be made in this game too. I assigned myself a task that involved a drive in the van to somewhere quiet, then pulled over on some country lane and called all the important people in my life to tell them the good news.

At one point during the job, Danny Allison actually took my hand in his and guided my mouse while I slipped into a catatonic state and almost cried. He saved me from a disastrous fall at the first hurdle.

I got the sign-off by about 4pm on the Thursday, which the council had let me swap for an extra day the following week. I sat there in what should surely be triumphant satisfaction, but felt like I had let Roger down. You're always your own worst critic, especially when the stakes are high. It was not my finest hour, but what I was yet to understand is that newspapers are realistic about the tight deadlines they give you. That work meant everything to me, but to them, it simply filled a space on one page for one day and would never be seen again unless it got them in legal trouble, so unless it was unthinkably rubbish, they would be satisfied and the job was considered a success. I went out first thing in the morning and bought eight copies of the paper. Though my parents were 100% supportive of everything I did, I think the first time they fully understood what I was attempting to do for a living was when I dropped that front cover on the kitchen table in front of them.

I planned my assault on the inbox and telephone of anyone who would listen, with news of my mega-client. Before I could get started, an email appeared on the screen. The art director of *The Guardian Sport* said she needed an illustration for the following Thursday edition's back page, one they hoped I could do. I fluttered off to cling to my power animal again, breathing deeply, eyes closed, rolling beneath their lids. Was this part of some Saturday night TV family stitch-up show? It wasn't and it turned out they had liked my *Film and Music* work for Roger and immediately demanded a piece of the action. Before I had the chance to start worrying that I had screwed up my big opportunity, I had my second *Guardian* commission in the bag.

I battered down the doors of all-and-sundry, holding my *Guardian* accolades aloft, like trophies of war. Illustration agents were sounded out about possible representation. Self-respect was a new notion in my career, but I started to feel a tiny note of it. You have to allow yourself a bit of pride here and there, otherwise, what's the point? These days, I am very mindful of the importance of enjoying the journey and process of any job, rather than stressing myself so silly by worrying about the end result, which always works out. Instead of peeking over the fence into Danny's glorious world, we were now both professional illustrators and the grass seemed a bit greener in my own kingdom.

Aside from the two *Guardian* jobs and another *WSC* outing, I was still financially reliant upon my council work. I had two credible clients on my CV and the people to whom I reached out started listening to me a little more. They don't know or care that you're spending £8 a week on food from Lidl, only that this guy has been 'doing stuff' for *The Guardian*.

Oddity raged in The Mill. Danny and I made a studio mascot, 'Milky Joe,' a character with a coconut as the head and a stick as the body, as seen on *The Mighty Boosh* TV show. A crack down the middle of the TV version of the coconut character formed the mouth and these little bushy leaves were used as eyebrows. For our version, we bought a cheap coconut from Lidl. His face was drawn with a marker pen and we used a ripped up old shirt for the dress, then stood him in the corner. By the end of the week, we were talking to Milky without a hint of humour. He never answered.

Sam Price was one of the first to surrender to my *Guardian*-touting phone calls, giving me work for *The Big Issue*; a weekly slot, £50 for each illustration in the South West England edition of the magazine. The guys at the Wales edition of the magazine used me a couple of times too, before they stopped publishing the title in Wales altogether. Sam's jobs only took me two or three hours each and further bolstered my CV. The mag ran a column by a vendor who had turned his life around for the better and I did the illustration for that. A rare shred of regularity provided a little security and that was very welcome.

NOTES ON WORKING FOR FREE

One of the problems with early freelance pressure is that you leave yourself wide open for the vultures with no budget. There are plenty of them out there; clients who know that for every creative who will not work for free, there are plenty who will.

Compromising financially is very damaging to the business. There's this long-standing perception of the arts, held by those outside of it, that its services should not be chargeable. The same people will not bat an eyelid about paying for a water cooler or a taxi on the company's tab, but if they need an artist? We're not sure we can justify paying for *that*.

Once someone has had something for free or very cheap, the value of that service is decreased in the same way you snatch up the 'buy-one-get-one-free' deals at Tesco and never return when the product offer ends. The vultures often use their reputation to seduce freelancers into working for free with their vast readerships and the otherwise unattainable experience that only they can provide. Charity, collaboration with other artists and skill swaps, are all valid avenues to channel your talents without payment and they come with creative freedom seldom found in commercial areas.

Right before *WSC* and *The Guardian* happened, I received an email from a mainstream culture magazine. They were overly friendly, complimentary and detailed the brief they had in mind for me, but at the foot of the email, they slipped in the killer detail. Unfortunately, there is no budget for this feature. I put the kettle on and fell quiet.

Danny sensed my dilemma hanging in the air and asked me what was wrong. I told him the score; that I was weighing up the possibility of doing the work without payment. After all, this was a major national publication, with a demographic I had not yet reached, and I had no other work to do at that point. Danny understood why it appeared an attractive proposition, after all he'd been there too, but he asked me if the magazine had any advertising in it.

Magazines, as a rule, are able to run largely thanks to the advertising within their pages which covers costs for production budgets, staff wages and more. He also asked me how long the job would take. It was a double page spread, so I said anywhere between two and three working days. My working days were rarely eight hours, usually a minimum of 10 and anywhere up to 16. He told me you have to consider what else I could do with those two days, for example, run with the two *Guardian* commissions and spend two days showing them off to prospective clients who *would* pay for my services.

It was a lot to think about and I crossed over the road to the garage shop to clear my head and take a look at the magazine. Riddled with advertisements and looking a little too well-produced to convince me that the 'no budget' claim held any credibility, I felt a little bit insulted. Turning them down, I set about marketing and 10 days later, in the space of a few hours, I was commissioned by two magazines to illustrate two lead features and they paid me a combined total of £650. One of those magazines would be where I met my girlfriend, Laura; who later became the art director!

I work for free when the client or project is a worthy one. If I have to drop my prices and do a deal, I highlight the discount on the invoice. Otherwise the clients will never pay more than the initial benchmark. For the good of the arts, you have to think beyond that next rent payment.

♦ROGER BROWNING: DESIGN DIRECTOR, *THE GUARDIAN NEWSPAPER*, 1995-2013

'I've definitely had more people offering me free work just to get into the paper. We don't want people to work for nothing. It's a case of feeling, morally, that that's wrong. Just because someone is desperate to get into the paper, it doesn't mean that we'll take free work. The relationship we have with an illustrator is one of negotiation. You come to me with an idea, I'll come back and give an opinion; so if someone is working for free, it is much harder to maintain that relationship – asking for amendments or retouches etc.'

FULL-TIME FREELANCE: TAKE TWO!

The council had done everything and more for me. Now I felt achingly ready for the time when I could dedicate all my time to my art, I started to think when might be a realistic time to try make my three-month trial a permanent fixture. January could be good? That would give me three months or so to prepare and I'd be all refreshed from Christmas. Springtime at the latest.

On the next Tuesday shift, I found out that the manager would be returning from her extended maternity leave and this meant the council crutch was kicked from under me.

One hour after this news, Sam called to say that the writer of my *Big Issue South West* columnist had 'gone missing'. There was no longer a column to illustrate. The columnist showed up eventually but discontinued his articles.

My two main streams of income had been cut in the space of 90 minutes. It felt like a hole had been sawn beneath my feet and down I fell, my eyes still in the room above for a moment, before following me with a comedy 'swooosh.' The £650 I had earned from the two commissions for a housing magazine and a management magazine now transformed from money I wanted to invest into my marketing and equipment, to survival money.

So here I was, coasting Tuesday, thrust into the wilds on Wednesday, like some sort of cruel wind up. I knew, deep down, that this was it, so tried to assure sympathetic council colleagues that I would take the blow as a blessing in disguise and not look back. On the inside, I was freaking right out.

On my penultimate shift, I had dropped off some recycling boxes at a family house when I had a call from an 'unknown number'. I had been to a Leeds United game at Elland Road sometime last season and, for the first time in a couple of years, picked up a copy of the club's glossy magazine, *Leeds, Leeds, Leeds*. Remaining folded in half in the back pocket storage in my jeans, it gathered dust for months before I finally decided to reach out to them. They had never used a single illustration in the magazine; I knew this because, since its inception in 1997, I had bought it every month without fail, to read and then chop up for my scrapbooks. So I naively assumed that they never would use any.

The call was from the publishing company which produced both the Leeds United club magazine and the official *Match Day Programme*. They had received my email only two days after discussing a full redesign for the new season. My timing had been an accidental master stoke. The editor had also seen my *Guardian Sport* illustration, which had been a football one, and liked what he saw, so unbeknownst to me, they were already aware of my existence. During the same phone call, they asked me to quote for a six-month contract and I waded in without thinking, buccaneer style, quoting a stupidly low fee. I had been reduced to a screeching child, mouth agape and completely spellbound by the prospect of working for my boyhood football club. They accepted my offer and I got straight on the phone to my dad who had taken me to watch Leeds as a child.

A lot had happened in the last few months and it was all quite overwhelming. I hadn't expected any of these breakthroughs so soon, but I'm constantly surprised by just how quickly the next level can become normality. Two dream clients were now on my CV. I had been kicked out of employment, into full-time freelance illustration.

I became more and more addicted to the rush of landing a new client and started to make more of a calculated nuisance of myself than ever before. I pestered agencies with more resolve, believing I could grow into a valuable asset for anyone, given the raw materials I possessed. I focused my efforts on the edgier sporting publications and editorial clients, even attempting to nominate myself for a specific feature or column illustration idea. It wasn't uncommon for me to try and suggest the editorial content myself, to create something I could illustrate!

I crafted a series of WWE superstar portraits as part of my ongoing obsession with the wrestling but the *WWE Magazine* published no contact details for their editorial team in the magazine and it was proving difficult to find them anywhere at all. Eventually I found a creative director from business-orientated social networking site LinkedIn, who accepted my invitation to connect.

IF YOU DON'T ASK...

Aside from the illustrations, Russell Brand's hilarious and whimsical *Articles Of Faith* columns in the Saturday edition of *The Guardian* had been another reason to part with £2 to buy the newspaper and I looked on with envy as illustrators created images for his weekly piece. I wasn't overawed by the artwork they used and really wanted the opportunity to have a go at it myself. I called up the sports art director and told her I would *love* to be given the opportunity to illustrate Russell's words. She consulted her diary and told me it was fully booked for the time being, but since I had asked her, the next time someone let her down, she'd be in touch.

Only two days later, I received a call asking if I wanted to save her bacon by illustrating this week's article. The buzz was incredible, proper adrenaline-flooding joy that had me jumping around in the studio. To this day, that job is my personal fast turnaround record; one I hope I never have to beat. They warned me that although my usual Guardian jobs carried tight deadlines, this was completely different, next level shit. Russell, they told me, was notorious for sending the entire place into chaos by filing the copy with no time at all for them to go to press. Whatever time remained, that would be how long I had to do the job and deliver the print-ready file.

At 6.05pm, it landed and left me with 50 minutes to think of an idea, sketch a rough, send it, wait on approval, craft the illustration, send the file and await final sign off. I shook throughout the whole 50 minutes, drawing then Tottenham Hotspur manager Harry Redknapp and made a guttural noise I have been unable to repeat since the file transfer displayed that green tick. I went straight out to the pub and got very drunk to decompress and celebrate.

I took my hangover to the newsagent the next morning and this time bought just one copy of the paper with my work next to Russell's bearded mugshot. It was one of the most satisfying feelings I have had to this day and I re-read the piece time and time again throughout the following week.

- Assume a potential client has no vision. Put things on a plate for them; put your work in their context and show them the example. They're busy people and don't have hours to decipher your work.

- If you don't ask, you don't get; be suggestive, cheeky, robust, opportunistic-but-nice and use your initiative.

- Do not assume that because someone is not already using your service, they will have no need for it. It may be that they just never thought of it, until you showed up.

- Potential contacts are everywhere, keep your eyes open and use your mobile phone, notepad or the back of your hand to log contact details until you can add them to your database.

- If you want something badly, show it. If you don't, there's someone with equal talent who will.

- Go and meet people, avoid digital dependency, human interaction remains crucial when developing trust in business.

- Treat everyone with the same high level of professionalism. A £50 cut-price deal for a friend should warrant the same level of respect as a major commission.

- Capitalize on any achievements and don't be afraid to flaunt them. People gain trust in you when they see others have published your work. Shout about it, really, really loudly at every opportunity, but be humble. Nobody likes an egotist.

- Choose your unpaid work carefully. Charities, skill swaps and personal projects are great channels to work for free. Vultures with hidden budgets will use you and, in the process, damage the value of the industry. Think about how long a free job would take, use that time to do more useful things, like marketing yourself to people who can pay you properly.

DIRTY FREUD: ELECTRONIC MUSICIAN, WRITER AND COMPOSER, BBC, WARNER, ROYAL EXCHANGE THEATRE.

'The way I made my first steps into making music came from one too many beers and a big mouth. I was in (Manchester nightclub) FAC251 drunkenly talking to one of the sound engineers and I started telling him I could DJ, easily. He just shook his head and laughed but after a couple more beers and me maintaining my claim, he said 'Ok, put your money where your mouth is. Have a go at it.' I remember waking up with my hangover and being filled with sheer panic, where was I going to learn?

By this point, we had good relationships with a few Manchester venues through my Quenched Music *reviews and after a few phone calls I managed to call in some favours. I'd spend four or five hours in the afternoon at venues that had the equipment I needed and didn't open their doors to the public until early evening. After I started to feel confident, I saved up for a Macbook and started to make my own beats. From there, I never looked back and I've supported big name DJs on tour and had a track chosen for the show reel of the director of* Breaking Bad. *When you're fortunate enough to find your passion, you have to let people know about your work, get in front of people and not let up.'*

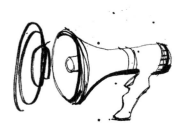

CHAPTER 8. AGENTS AND REPRESENTATION

What does a creative agent do? I didn't know a great deal about them. Six illustration agencies had been receiving my work on a regular basis, without much of a response. Considering I really liked the idea of being able to tell someone they would have to talk to my agent, I had no knowledge of what they could do for me professionally.

Danny's representation by Illustration Ltd, he told me, basically meant they advised when you needed advice, promoted you to potential clients, sorted the official stuff and priced work, taking a percentage of the fee upon payment for the job. This sounded attractive to me as I was earning a bare minimum wage through my own representation and felt like I needed some heavyweight support. Rich Taylor also pointed out that representation was more than just someone to promote your work, it was also an endorsement of your professional quality, much the same as a musician signing to a decent record label. Aside from the morning after the Russell Brand commission, I certainly didn't feel or behave like a rock star, but representation was an encouraging idea nonetheless.

I signed with Illustration Ltd not long after Danny had clued me up. For six months or so, I had been sending work to their contact address to no avail. He had since put in a good word and my work had been steadily improving. It was a total no brainer to sign with the world's biggest illustration agency. They said they had been keeping an eye on my progress, that my recent technical improvements had been impressive and they thought the relationship could be mutually beneficial if I continued to develop at the same rate.

You have to be careful with agents. As with anything else, there are good ones and there are cowboys. Luckily for me I had heard nothing but glowing reviews of Illustration Ltd from Danny, who had a year or two's experience of working with them. You'll hear stories detailing some agents demanding that you must put all work through them, even your own clients that you worked hard and invested your own money to attain when you were alone in the wilderness. Confirm all terms of anything you sign in writing and have it looked at by someone who knows about media-based contracts. Some will try to tie you to quite unfair contracts. Written legal documents are necessary for the protection of both parties, but I don't agree with the 'we want everything you have' policy and Illustration Ltd respected that, which embedded crucial early trust in the relationship. We agreed to test the water with an informal understanding to see how things progressed.

VICTORIA PEARCE: FORMER FASHION AND PHOTOGRAPHY AGENT, CURRENT AGENT AT ILLUSTRATION LTD

'We currently represent approximately 200 artists worldwide. I moved from a very small agency at Pearce-Stoner Associates, where we represented 13 people, so at first I was quite overwhelmed by the scale of Illustration Ltd. The thing with illustration is, we are representing artists of different genres, styles and techniques. I like to think of us as the Selfridges of illustration. Kind of like you come in the front door and turn left to menswear, or go upstairs to contemporary womenswear. Hopefully, what unites all the talent within the family is the quality of the work. This enables us to work for a very diverse set of clientele, internationally.

My role is marketing and communications, so I come up with ideas for e-newsletters and printed materials. We temporarily put print marketing on hold, but I felt that everyone was becoming overloaded with e-communications, so there remains something special about receiving something physical that is beautifully designed and well thought out in your post box. That can really stand out.

Based on a conversation with one of our illustrators, Paul Holland, I came up with an idea to launch the 'scrapbook' marketing e-newsletter; a newsletter with Q & A interview features and a free downloadable PDF high resolution poster of their artwork. The idea was that we'd showcase the inspirations, ideas and influences of our artists. It was a big hit so we rolled it out as a printed notebook, part blank so the client could actually write on the blank pages, *but also containing editorial features on interesting projects our talent had worked on. We've just sent out the eighth scrapbook.*

The lead feature is about Dreamland, which was at one time, the biggest seaside amusement park in the country. It's going to be opening again in 2015 as Britain's first ever amusement park of thrilling historic rides. All the glorious iconography, typography and imagery that comes with the old amusement parks is iconic and it coincided with Sarah Beetson, one of our artists, taking up a three-month artist residency at Coney Island. Coney Island it turns out, was the original inspiration for Dreamland, in Margate. The scrapbook has generated some fantastic interaction with clients, in person and on social media. I'm also thrilled that this edition, the eighth in the on-going series, is on sale at Dreamland's Visitor Centre (to help raise funds for the DL Trust), The House of Illustration and the Rizzoli Bookshop at Somerset House.'

MOVING TO THE CITY

Our time in Oyston Mill came to an end around late spring 2009. We had eyed potential replacements for the departing members, but when Danny Allison announced he needed a change of scene and would be heading for an adventure in Australia, it felt like time to leave. We worked from his house, which had a spare room, for the next few months. We spent so long in the same room, that the prospect of losing his company and wisdom seemed increasingly like losing a limb to me. We had even bought three goldfish for the space and would now have to work out custody arrangements.

One quiet afternoon, Leona, his girlfriend, had walked across the upstairs landing and glanced in the bathroom to see us washing the fish tank, topless, given the baking summer heat. The tank was hidden from view and she thought we were washing one another. Her lack of surprise was unsettling.

We bought second-hand bicycles and every day at 7pm, we habitually rode down to Morrisons supermarket and fill a bag with cut-price sandwiches and cakes. It was a bit embarrassing, sitting there with a cup of tea, watching the fridges like hawks. They knew our game and sometimes delayed the stickering to watch us squirm. Other times, the older ladies took a kind of motherly pity on us and priced them down early.

To say that freelancing in insular conditions can have a detrimental effect on your state of mind would be an understatement. One afternoon, we returned from a lunchtime trip to Morrison's to find dog mess on the pavement outside Danny's house. He was spitting blood, swearing about whoever kept letting their 'f**king dog shit' outside his house. He then put the supermarket deli bag over his hand, ready to pick up the offending stool. I found the image of him, standing there trembling, red in the face, completely hilarious, so took out my camera phone and captured the moment.

For a few months, we'd been caught up in an image-editing war, which involved adding our heads or faces into funny, sordid or weird images and posting them on social media. It was a game of one-upmanship that got out of hand, a complete misuse of our skills. It would eventually get me banned from Facebook for a month. Despite compositing him into blatant pornography, the 'shit on the pavement' incident was the fuse that lit him up in a fit of rage, the only time in the ten years we've been friends, that I can ever recall him reacting to any form of rib. We stood there, arguing in the street like children. It continued inside the house, where I uploaded the photo to my computer, thinking he would see the funny side.

He didn't and rapidly downloaded a photo of a girl I quite liked at the time, placing both of our heads onto a hardcore porn image. He locked it in a password-protected folder and swore that if the dog shit photo ever saw light of day, he would not hesitate to release this in the public domain, where not only the girl in question, but numerous clients would see me, all tanned, toned and doing unspeakable things. We were losing our ability to focus and his decision to move to Australia saved us from spiralling out of control and into some kind of Hunter S Thompson adventure.

By this time, I had started to bring in a reasonable amount of regular work. *The Times Education Supplement* brought me unexpected repeat business, responding to my monthly updates two years on from my initial visit to London to see them, rewarding my persistency. The Russell Brand *Guardian* gig had become a monthly slot alongside my ongoing work for other areas of the newspaper.

On one occasion, I did a job on location, in *The Guardian's* Farringdon offices. I was in the city and they asked me to work at short notice. I had no scanner with me and stuck my neck out, asking if they had any kit I could use. They laughed but said yeah and I sat there, feeling like I'd been permitted to go backstage, wandering round the place all covert, seeing how this chaotic national newspaper world operated.

I started to look into the possibility of a move to London, given how many of my clients were there and how much I enjoyed my promotional visits. The living costs dwarfed my £9k first year of freelancing income and although some people had been living at The Hootenanny, I didn't fancy taking up a permanent residence there. A freelance living can fluctuate wildly without any notice and if London backfired it could be terminal at such a fragile early stage of my career. There's always fear that eventually has to be ignored to progress, but with this one, a few quick calculations confirmed that, mathematically, it just wasn't going to happen.

I viewed flats in Leeds; for their familiarity I suppose. Then one night, a drunken friend called from overseas travels to check in and slurred abuse at me when I mentioned West Yorkshire. She had studied in Manchester and suggested it was a much better location for my line of work.

MANCHESTER HAS EVERYTHING EXCEPT A BEACH

All I knew about Manchester was Oasis, The Stone Roses and the two football teams. The red one had given me too much grief over the previous 20 years. Stone Roses frontman Ian Brown was quoted on T-shirts as having said 'Manchester had everything except a beach'. That sounded pretty tempting. Beaches are best left for holidays anyway.

Danni Skerritt was a Londoner who had lived two floors above me in the university halls of residence. We had the odd passing chat and we had made up the numbers on each other's football teams here and there, but aside from that, we didn't know each other. I hadn't seen him for six months or so since a chance encounter in the street, when he had told me he was enjoying Manchester and his writing.

I couldn't tell you why I called him one rainy Tuesday evening. I was walking home from Danny Allison's place after work one day and Skerritt popped into my head, unannounced, the way people sometimes do when you're walking alone. I'd always had his number in my phone in case I needed a footballer. On the off chance he was on the same number and could paint a picture of Manchester for me, I dialled him. I told him I was thinking about Manchester as a living option and hoped he could tell me what it was like to live and work there.

He delayed in responding, then muttered, 'Easy Ben, I can't really talk, but I need to find somewhere in Manchester to live, by next week. Do you want to come over this Friday and have a look around?' I paused for a second and thought about it. Sometimes you don't really have time to consider and the gut instinct just has to be trusted. I took a leap of faith with nothing to lose and arranged to meet him at Deansgate train station at 10am on the Friday. By 11.30 we had signed for a flat in Whalley Range, South Manchester.

Skerritt would later tell me he was squatting and had just put his phone on charge in the university library. He'd started to turn his back when the phone rang and he was confused when my name showed. I had never once called him before then. He'd been on this trip to the east that fell somewhere between an 18-30s holiday and a soul-searching pilgrimage. He said he had discovered some Indian modification of hedonism and taken leave of his senses after riding the Siberian Express to China.

Discovering this new way of thinking had blown him apart and he eventually washed ashore in Manchester with his mind in his backpack. Rather than go home and borrow money from his parents, he had opted to squat, while he completed his writing scholarship. Drifting and a lack of stability had grown tiring, so when I had called, he decided to gamble and see if I was game for a fresh start under a rented roof. He'd been showering in gyms and charging his phone in the university library where he still had alumni membership.

I felt uncertain at first, but the first flat we viewed was reasonably priced, in a leafy suburb and there was something about him that I liked, though I couldn't quite put my finger on what this was. Maybe it was the fact that, what started as a football conversation, had gone on to reveal a mutual love of wrestling. I tested him with questions about Summerslam 1992, Mr McMahon's Royal Rumble win in 1999 and asked if he had seen that week's episode of WWE Smackdown. Not only did he answer all correctly, he elaborated on all three questions. Anyone who was squatting and somehow keeping up with wrestling programmes was going to command my respect. I was always going to sign that tenancy agreement.

I settled in quite quickly despite the meltdown each time my rent left the account, now double the amount I had paid in Preston. Manchester was still small enough to pop round to a friend's house for a cup of tea, but there were galleries, gigs and nightlife in abundance. I knew a few people in the city and Rich Taylor's parting gift from Preston was a phone number for a shared co-operative office set up called 'Openspace' in which he thought I might be interested. Three years after his magical apparition in Preston, he was sending me on my way with yet another priceless contact. I called the number and recognized the voice. It was one of the guys from UHC who had given me my first commission in 2006. He now co-ran Openspace and invited me down to take a look. The deal was: if you joined as a member, the monthly rate was £100 instead of £150. My membership gave me the reduced £100 tab in return for a few hours' work each month. Every member had a responsibility in the co-op. My role was to show prospective tenants around the space and sort out keys for them. This was all-inclusive and the space was really cool. It was in Hulme, a part of Manchester that was pretty vibrant in the 1970s and '80s, Openspace was right next to where Manchester photographer Kevin Cummins had shot that iconic Joy Division image on the snowy bridge and was nestled in the middle of a housing co-operative, with a bohemian little café/bar nextdoor, perfect for meetings or a place to sketch and think. The place even had an undercover outdoor area where I could get messy with my paints.

Danny Allison came over a week before he departed for Australia and shot my press photograph, something I had only just started to think about the value of commissioning. He had a photography degree and had worked for the *Blackpool Gazette* before switching to illustration. Continuing photography as a hobby, his shots packed the same punch that his artwork did and I loved it. He did this for me without charge, since we were close friends, on the simple condition that I trusted his direction. After all, he knew me better than most and said it needed to get my personality over to the viewer. I had this curly mop of hair at the time, so he stuck a load of pencils and pens in it and stood on a chair above me. I looked up and he took the photo. I love that image and still use it from time to time. I had started to think about my overall brand, not just my portfolio and the importance of strong presentation in every area of my business, especially in a city as stylish and competitive as Manchester was becoming obvious. Most people buy into artists and musicians as much for the mystique and person behind the work, for the work itself.

Skerritt and I watched an obscene amount of wrestling and sometimes he'd hang out at the studio with me. He stuck a load of his poetry on the walls of the flat and made me a few mix-tapes in an effort to broaden my music horizons. I stuck up a few illustrations and allowed him access to my WWE VHS collection, which I had been dragging around with me since I left my family home, despite technology leaving video tapes behind. Living with him started to prove something of a cultural apprenticeship. He was a Londoner after all, and knew about cool things like chime music, rare Marvel™ comics and films I had never heard of. His stories of travel blew my mind and I wanted adventure too.

My client list grew steadily with *Manchester City FC* magazine and *Design Week* coming on board. Man City's magazine was produced by the same publishing house as Leeds United, for whom I was still working each month and they too wanted a piece of my football illustration. Sam Freeman had been the art director at the *Big Issue* before Sam Price and we had met when I went to London for the second time, keeping in touch since. I had been out for beers with the *Big Issue* staff. Freeman had joined us. He told me to come and see him in his new role at *Design Week* before I went home. I did and he gave me a regular illustration slot in their opinion column.

Preston's creative community had been something of a clique. Outside of it, you didn't really exist. I found it frustratingly insular. The thing with small towns is that their local kings and queens enjoy a degree of celebrity among their court, so they are reluctant to jeopardize that by welcoming newcomers. Manchester had film, theatre, slam poetry, art, music and sport all going on and each area was more accessible given its larger scale. The buzz of being in a major city like this was having a hugely positive effect on my self-confidence and creative output.

Openspace Studios housed about 12 different businesses and I began to pick up work just by being in the space, including some charity work for Mines Advisory Group. Youth Discovery Ventures rented the desk next to mine and they worked with disadvantaged young people through art and sport. I branded the company, a voluntary job that won me *Creative Match's* 'Flair Illustrator of the Month' award.

Skerritt and I concocted a preposterous goal system in order to keep us grounded and driven. It would have been easy to start developing an ego with clients like Manchester City and *Design Week* and you do see it happen to people, but we both talked about long-term goals and our ambition transcended simply attaining big client names on a CV.

The ranking system was a hierarchical ladder of WWE wrestlers, past and present. We laid down markers, achievements we would have to earn in our world that we could equate to a 'championship' victory in wrestling. I know, it's pathetic, right? But we got childishly excited about it and used the system to great effect when the days were tough. 'What would the heavyweight champ, John Cena think about you 'just popping on a wash load' mid-afternoon when you could be making promotional phone calls?' 'What would

I have to do to elevate myself to the level of former wrestler turned movie star, Dwayne 'The Rock' Johnson?'

Spending lots of time with Danny Allison had really enhanced my verbal skills. He was pretty streetwise and I learned much from him. This worked well in London. The northern accent stood out in many meetings and my early fear that people would simply fail to understand me proved unfounded; it seemed to go in my favour and people would often reference it to thaw what could have been an awkward introduction. It made new friendships easier to come by in the hostels, just because you had the old 'where are you from?' conversation so often. Slowly building relationships with clients was something of a perfect counter to the disheartening amount of artistic talent in my industry.

I called up the editor of *Leeds, Leeds, Leeds* one day and asked if there was any way of featuring me in the club magazine. I got along well with him and highlighted the fact that they were paying me slightly below average for my work and I was a lifelong obsessive fan. It was completely tongue-in-cheek but, deep down, I'd played out this kind of scenario a thousand times in my head. He laughed and said he'd try get me some column inches, but no promises. I answered interview questions and, in the next issue, there was my new press shot, my mop of hair dominating two thirds of a double-paged spread with a pull quote about my childhood encounter with club legend, David Batty. Kelly Jones from Stereophonics, also a life long Leeds fan got only a single page in that issue, which is ridiculous.

The magazine arrived through the door of friends from Keighley who received a copy as part of their club memberships and they were straight on the phone, asking what the hell I was doing in their Leeds United magazine. My dad took it into work and showed it around; to see him proud like that is still one of the biggest rewards of my career thus far.

Work was almost non-existent with my agency, Illustration Ltd and I had started to worry they may drop me from the roster before we even had chance to get started.

In September, I was contacted by a London-based collective called Inky Goodness. They asked me if I'd like to take part in an exhibition they were organizing; 50 artists and illustrators each hand-painted their work onto a skateboard deck. This would be my first exhibition since New Blood in 2006 so I couldn't wait to head down and flutter around a gallery on Brick Lane, pretending to be important.

The show came around and I checked in for a few nights at The Hootenanny. No fruit machine raids took place this time and the staff forgave the boozy antics of my earlier visit. We had been sent word that a couple of guys, one of them a director from Channel 4, would be visiting the show with a view to recruiting artists to exhibit some work at a show they would soon be curating at their home in Crystal Palace, south east London. Halfway through the evening, I noticed a swarm of swooning artists crowding around two guys, attempting to woo them. Wandering the space, I pondered how I might avoid being forgotten forever, which would inevitably happen amongst the throng. There are only so many people you can meet and remember in one night.

The rush died down and people seemed to be leaving around 10pm so I headed over and chatted to the two guys. They were very friendly and seemed more relaxed now that things had quieted down, excited about putting on their own show. I had to know what the deal was. I found out that people were invited to drop their work at the house, any time the next day. Thinking on my feet, I asked what time the director finished working at Channel 4. I asked if it would be cool to come and meet him after work at their headquarters and head to the house in his company. He looked a little surprised, but I told him I did not know how to get there and that it would be nice to chat anyway. I left him with a business card and said I'd see him tomorrow, taking his number with me. I was operating on adrenaline alone and, in truth, I was a little nervous simply knowing that Channel 4 did some pretty cool creative work and here was a chance to hopefully chat a little more than the 'hi!' and 'bye" that the drop off would allow me.

The next day, I just about navigated my way to the impressive Channel 4 building on Horseferry Road in London, with huge art installations outside. I called the director. He came to meet me and showed me around the headquarters, taking me through the broadcasting suites and the studios where they put together Channel 4's programming and promotions. I loved it, seeing all these people in little rooms with lots of lights, making television, even if I did have the previous night's skateboard artwork, covered in some rather hellish looking drawings, under my arm.

We jumped on the bus to Crystal Palace and talked the whole way. Upon arriving, I noticed that most of the other exhibiting artists had been and gone, leaving their work.

I dropped off my skateboard deck for the show, which would be in a month or so's time.

They happened to have made too much food that night and kindly asked if I wanted to stay for dinner. This big Alsatian dog padded around the place, which I pestered a lot. The food was delicious and it was pretty cool to be dining with a Channel 4 director and a professional architect. During the dinner, the director started laughing. He then said, 'Ben, Tyson v Thatcher...What the hell?!'

When I was working from his spare room, Danny Allison had been tickled by the 'Race v Sex challenge' illustration of Obama and Clinton. This triggered the same boyish attraction to the thunderous reactions my drawings of teachers at school would receive, so I ran with the idea and drafted a new poster called 'Tallon v Allison, Illustration Deathmatch' picturing us facing off against one another. Danny was drawn with a toilet seat around his neck, beer in hand. This spawned a whole set, that I called, 'The Versus Series'. Beyond those four walls and feeding our increasingly twisted sense of humour, I saw no other value in the project. Some were uploaded to my online portfolio to provide a touch of quirkiness and I was shocked when *Computer Arts Magazine*, a major arts publication across the UK and Europe, asked if they could run a feature on the project.

In the few words I gave *CA* about the piece, I got excited and promised that the series finale would be, 'Tyson v Thatcher, First Blood Match.' I delivered on my promise and now this Channel 4 director was laughing at the dinner table, over the resultant poster.

Three weeks later, I took a call from him. The Versus Series had stayed in his thoughts and, if I was interested, he had a 30-second TV trailer to put together for the new season of *Skins*, which would be airing on E4 from November 2009. He wanted me to illustrate it, in a style very close to the Tyson v Thatcher work! I distinctly remember that I was swinging from some metal bars that formed part of the housing co-op's structure, round the back of Openspace when I took that call, waiting for my spray paint to dry. I climbed down and sat on a wooden crate. Aside from the occasional charity brief and a shoddy CD sleeve design I had done back in Preston, here was my first commission outside of editorial design and it would be airing to a national audience on primetime television. Wow! I had no idea how to animate my style, but the guys I would be working with assured me that they would pair me with an experienced animator who could walk me through the process of bringing my static illustrations to life.

The *Skins* job opened up many doors into new markets for my work. Until this point, animation of my work had not felt remotely possible, but I worked with experienced professionals who were very patient with me throughout. The arts publications ran some positive press on the job and my social media following went up a great deal after an army of teenagers followed me when Channel 4 posted about my trailer. I pandered to every one of their compliments, revelling in my glimmer of limelight. I was a digital tart for a few days, having all of this, in case it never happened again! The money was better than my editorial rates and I was out of my overdraft for the first time since university.

Things were looking up. Skerritt had some plays showing at the Everyman Theatre in Liverpool and The Royal Exchange in

Manchester. He was now working as a part time projectionist at the Odeon cinema. We agreed that if things continued to improve, we would be eyeing a tag-team championship match on our progress chart.

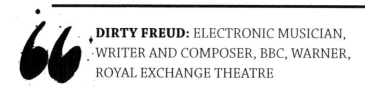

DIRTY FREUD: ELECTRONIC MUSICIAN, WRITER AND COMPOSER, BBC, WARNER, ROYAL EXCHANGE THEATRE

'It was only into my late 20s that I set up Quenched Music with Ben because we both wanted to apply our skills to the music industry. With confidence we gave each other, we thought it was worth a shot, giving it a name and a website and very quickly I started to learn that if you want something, you have to just go for it. It's there for the taking. I have no academic qualifications in sound engineering, DJing or making music, but here I am, somehow doing all those things.

If you hold the music I make now up to the things they teach on academic courses, I'd be breaking too many rules. Very quickly, these ideas that make my sound original and personal to me, would have been shot down or moulded into something that everyone could understand. The problem is, my electro-dub doesn't abide to the rulebook under electronica or classical music, but somehow it works, it's me.'

- Agents can be very useful, but they are difficult to acquire and not all have wholesome intentions. Do your research and check what you are signing ten times over.

- Photo-editing skills can be dangerous. Posting things classed as 'pornography' on Facebook can earn you a ban, without warning, no matter how funny you and your peers find your sordid creations.

- If you're stifled in a place, move on. A change of scenery is a healthy way to keep the ideas and inspiration flowing.

- Don't give up on potential clients. An old tutor of mine was commissioned after a client saw some work he'd done 15 years earlier and went on to become a well-paying regular. Many people mean it when they say they have you on file.

- Your overall brand is important. Call upon friends with skills you don't possess and work out a skill swap or favour to build a polished look. Photos, short films, bios and blogs all allow potential clients to get closer and understand what you're about.

- Tandem goals and targets with friends and peers can help keep you both motivated. The tough times are a little easier with someone by your side.

- People tend to remember things that make them laugh or challenge them in some way. Personal work and insular projects are often a better way of achieving this than the standard commercial jobs.

- Be aware of other uses for your work. Your style could apply to many markets you never thought about.

CHAPTER 9. WIDENING HORIZONS

Since I discovered Blur and their frontman, Damon Albarn, my cravings to work in music had never really gone away. It was just that I didn't really have the opportunities to do it and my priorities were elsewhere during my time in Keighley and Preston.

My flatmate Danni Skerritt's musical teachings triggered new curiosity in me and I wanted to know who these new artists were, where they were from, what type of music they played and how I could work with some of them.

Local gigs were plentiful in the Manchester, so we became regular fixtures at the music venues, particularly Gullivers, an old school pub and a complete contrast to the trendy Northern Quarter bars that surrounded it.

Attending these gigs was affordable because Manchester's three universities ensured cheap mid-week drinks offers were numerous all over the city. We'd go out, watch some music, get pissed for a fiver and feel really old, surrounded by 18-year-olds licking each other's faces on nightclub dance floors, then stumble home. We started befriending some of the local bands we had been watching and discovered really talented outfits. The thing with musicians is, you get some who work really hard, appreciate the need for a lot of patience along the way and make clever decisions. Others get a sniff of attention and spend their time honing their hair, buying retro jewellery and wearing really long shoes, waiting for fame and fortune to come their way, then quit when it doesn't. The Manchester music scene was swamped with lots of both, all vying for gigs and management.

Danni Skerritt spent more time with the bands than I did and he headed down to a night that the lads from a local gypsy punk outfit had heard about at a pub called the Thirsty Scholar, underneath the arches by Oxford Road train station. The pub was a grotto of sorts, with graffiti on the walls, overflowing cigarette bins on the outer walls and there always seemed to be middle-aged metal heads skulking around the place.

A guy called 'Tuesday Tony,' who we had heard was rubbish on all other days of the week, ran a night where rumour had it that, if you were a decent musician, you could get paid to play. Skerritt headed down with the band. He had studied creative writing and wanted to try his hand at journalism in order to get closer to the music scene. He approached Tuesday Tony and offered to review his live night. With cider as payment, Skerritt set up a blog for his reviews. He called it 'Quenched', a reference to the deal they struck. He reviewed the first night for the blog. No form of payment ever materialized, so neither the band nor Skerritt returned to the Thirsty Scholar. Instead, he took up an offer from a different and more prominent local promoter to come and review his nights in the city centre.

The logo Skerritt cobbled together for the Quenched blog was bright purple and vomit brown, like something an eight-year-old would put together in Microsoft Word, and he put a clip-art pint glass on it, with no suggestion whatsoever of music; the key subject matter. I kept an eye on what he was doing. Despite the logo, I'd been impressed by the standard of new music coming out of Manchester and his growing knowledge about it made me think it would be worth forgiving his art sins in order to collaborate.

I told him, during a walk to town one day, that if we combined our skills, we could offer a unique skill-set to musicians and industry folk. He was keen on the idea and I wasted no time in putting together a new logo. The purple pint glass had become a regular feature in my nightmares. The result wasn't my finest hour, just two illustrated fish and the words 'Quenched Unsigned,' but it would do for now. Suddenly I had a second business on my hands.

We never had a plan for Quenched. I just figured that I would stand a better chance of one day achieving my goal to work on album sleeves with good musicians if I approached the task under a company banner, rather than as a lone freelancer. I assigned myself the role of creative director, so that if a sleeve wasn't a good fit for my illustration style, I could source someone who was closer to the mark and take a cut of the fee while furthering my art direction skills and CV. It sounded pretty cool too. Skerritt would write bios and any press packs. The reviews would be our method of attracting music professionals and fans to our website, which we paid my web designer friend to build; he cut us a good deal. I had recently commissioned him to replace my first personal website which I had hammered out during my early days in the Stables and brought him in to work with us here. Quenched was always going to be a slow burner, something into which I could invest a little of the money that I had saved from my illustration, to try move things forward on a broader scale.

Skerritt came into my room one Saturday morning. He lay down next to me and my latest *Guardian* hangover, on my bed. This was now the norm; we'd grown really close and our friendship made the crucial honesty needed in business much easier to wield. He told me about an event that was taking place in Macclesfield, called 'Unconvention Factory'.

Skerritt had met Jeff Thompson, one of the directors of Unconvention, up at the Gullivers open mic night, which he had now started to run, on occasion. I designed a little flyer for it and we named it 'Acoustic Broth'. The night gave him the opportunity to find out about the local music talent and to shadow the sound engineer, learning how everything worked. He said that although we didn't have a finished website or even a business card yet, we could at least email Jeff's Unconvention and see if they might let us attend the event. The tickets were expensive and though worth the fee, unaffordable for us. The only way we could go to Unconvention was under guise of press or media. We didn't even know what the event was about, but we had no plans the following Saturday, so wrote a ridiculously overly-impassioned email, stating why we deserved a place at the event. Somehow it worked and they placed us on the press list.

DIRTY FREUD: ELECTRONIC MUSICIAN, WRITER AND COMPOSER, BBC, WARNER, ROYAL EXCHANGE THEATRE.

'Where I grew up in north London on the estates, it could get pretty dangerous when the lights went out. Gun violence, knife crime, just regular people looking to take things from you. As a consequence of that, you'd have different rappers, like Kano and Wiley. Dizzee Rascal would come down and they'd all battle. They'd rap about people trying to jack you for your trainers and suddenly I had positive role models, channelling the things I went through, to make cool music. It's about that personal connection and art keeps people out of trouble, but more importantly, it made me believe I could do something with my life and supported my recent confidence that I could make my own music. There are many bumps in the road, but you have to trust, work hard and get along with people and above all else, I love this.'

FORCING CONVERSATIONS

Unconvention Factory was an all-day event. The plan was, 10 artists would record and produce a whole album in one day. You had 30 minutes to record a track, 30 minutes to go backstage and produce it. There would also be a number of debates and discussion panels about various music industry topics. I'd become quite consumed with Quenched Unsigned and wanted to make my mark in music. I just didn't know what that mark would be. I believe one of the keys to long-term success is consolidating your success while you're ahead.

Sitting upstairs on the balcony, watching everyone arrive at Unconvention, we had expected only industry players to attend and had come here to chat to them in the hope that some of them might drink too much free booze, and that valuable things about the music industry might fall out of their mouths.

Reverend and The Makers are one of my favourite bands, a Sheffield-based indie/electro five-piece with a debut album I have played far too much. At 6'6 or thereabouts, with a thick South Yorkshire accent, their frontman, Jon McClure, is an unmistakable presence in any room and I immediately recognized him, grabbing Skerritt by the arm and pointing to him. When he vanished from sight, I insisted that we track him down. We found him outside having a cigarette and struck up conversation. He was very friendly and within five minutes we were discussing racism in the music industry among other heavy topics. His band would be one of the artists on the one-day album and he was a guest on one of the panels, later in the afternoon.

I asked if he would mind answering a few impromptu questions and he obliged, forcing me into conducting my first ever interview. I made notes on my mobile phone that I would later write up, as I was completely unprepared for this. Interviewing one of my favourite musicians seemed total madness to me, and we would now have an exclusive for the Quenched website when it launched. It was a different buzz to the thrill illustration achievements gave me and I was instantly hooked by the diversity that two disciplines offered.

It didn't take us long to notice the backstage area for Unconvention artists and panellists. Our passes did not permit us to enter, but we chatted to the people on the door for a little while and then took advantage of someone interrupting us, diverting their attention as we slipped in. We expected to be thrown out at any moment, but stayed close to others at all times, using them as human shields, and gathered as many email contacts as we could. Converse sponsored Unconvention and there were free pairs of these cool new white hi-top shoes for the artists, but we were abruptly halted when we tried our luck.

I didn't recognize many faces but then why would I? I was an illustrator with next to no knowledge of music. Skerritt was chatting to a guy who was sat in the corner of the room and had the longest dreadlocks I had ever seen; they reached the floor when his hat was off. I wandered over with a packet of bourbon biscuits that the organizers had laid on, along with a pot of tea from the same table and offered him a snack. He declined. 'Tea?' 'No, thanks mate.' I caught Skerritt's eyes, which were bulging and trembling at me, telepathically screaming, 'WHAT THE F**K ARE YOU DOING?' His gritted teeth confirmed he was being serious here.

Recoiling, I went to the toilet, clearly out of my depth. When I came back, Skerritt told me that the guy was Don Letts, a DJ, filmmaker and musician who was one of the main DJ purveyors of punk and reggae music, part of the reason it exploded onto the UK scene in the 1970s.

Skerritt had grown up idolizing the guy thanks to his parents' love of his work. I've heard that Don had infamously sneaked into Bob Marley's hotel room after he'd played a gig and spent the night talking to him. In the same fashion, we had made our way backstage, unpermitted and chatted to

Don, even if I had been more focused on the tea and biscuits. I thought he was the coolest bastard in town when he laughed at my question, 'Do you have a business card we could take?' and replied, 'I've come this far without one, I'm not about to start now, I'm not a hard man to find.'

We asked him for an email address and he obliged. He would later grant us an interview to go with our Jon McClure piece in which he told us, 'When your work becomes your play, you've reached the peak of civilization.' In a haphazard sequence of events, we had bagged our first noteworthy content for Quenched Unsigned.

Quenched also enabled Skerritt to get pretty good at the sound engineering. We were making no money through our project, but it had given us a vehicle to bring in opportunities that were unreachable individually. He continued his new habit of learning things on the job by convincing Factory 251, the new incarnation of legendary Manchester venue, The Haçienda, to let us put on a Quenched band night at the venue. We had never done this before and he somehow managed to evade the question, 'Where else have you promoted gigs?' on three occasions. I designed the posters and Skerritt recruited the bands. We then split the costs of the door entry fee of £4 per person. We always lost money on these nights, but it got people into the building and spread the Quenched name. The bassist from Gorillaz turned up at one night.

THE IMPORTANCE OF SIMPLICITY

When you freelance, there's no sick pay and I had to do a *Guardian Sport* job at the height of a fever. I'm not talking man flu; this was struggling-to-walk-and-cold-sweat-hallucination ill. I somehow managed it and the piece I churned out through barely open eyes was the one that I consigned straight to the hard drive alumni and forgot about. In a strange twist, I was invited to teach at Central Saint Martins College and I later found out it was the fever-fuelled work that brought me to their attention. Teaching was a welcome addition to illustration and Quenched and a chance to interact with humans. Any geek loves the opportunity to share their poison of choice with anyone and it paid quite well.

Harry Lyon-Smith has been the director at Illustration Ltd for more than 20 years. He is a great bloke with boat-loads of experience. I called him to discuss my situation at the agency. Despite engineering the job through my own channels prior to signing with the agency, I had put the *Skins* job through them since I had no idea how to price anything accurately outside of editorial illustration and they had started to bring me the odd editorial job by this time, so I wanted to build a relationship on mutual trust. But these jobs were mere coughs and splutters, there was no roar of a purring engine yet and I still feared they might shed me at any time. I asked Harry if he had any pointers or suggestions that might help me bring in some bigger jobs. I liked the idea of rates that advertising could bring, being quite a lucrative market. But where did I start?

Harry explained to me that I had to treat my agency portfolio as a shop window. If it was cluttered and too busy, it would be hard to digest. Images in context are useful as they demand less thinking and can be easily understood by the viewer. My marketing methods so far had been 'smash and grab'. Make a call, act on instinct, hustle, pester, demand. Illustration Ltd had the most-visited illustration site on the web, which meant that thousands of eyes were seeing the site each day.

The trouble was, you could only speculate about the kind of work that might attract people to your profile and what they were looking for.

It was almost as if I could put what I wanted in my store window, but never leave the shop. The potential customers had to come in before I could see or speak to them. Suddenly it made sense. The vast majority of my work was conceptual, owing to its place on the pages of magazine and newspaper articles. This meant it was clever, but not instant or informative about where else the style might be applied outside of editorial design. I had assumed that advertising and new media clients would have the time and vision to decode this work and apply it to their product's context. Not the case. Why would they when they could sift through thousands of instantly gratifying portfolios that did not require any deduction? 'Simplify your work! If you want to attract mobile companies, where are the illustrations of phones?' Harry said to me.

His simple advice made sense and here I was, facing another portfolio overhaul. I got off the phone and immediately kicked off my Adidas Forest Hills trainers, photographed them and spent three hours working up simple observational illustrations. The results were colourful, vibrant and not cryptic or over-elaborate. There was something more fun about owning the piece stylistically, without spending hours sketching concepts. I uploaded them to my portfolio as Harry suggested and set about some more subject matter.

I doubt I'll ever see such rapid results ever again, but one week later, I was invited to Next Plc's Tottenham Court Road offices. The clothing company was interested in commissioning me to create illustrations on a large scale to be printed as murals in their London stores, specifically in the children's shoes department. The Adidas mock-ups had been in my portfolio for only a week and now this, Harry's words still ringing in my ears. I was certain the job would fall through, which often happens in the advertising world, given the stakes and the numbers of people you have to please. I signed the job confirmation form and made more money from that job than I had in three month's worth of editorial commissions.

OF TAX AND ACCOUNTANTS

Freelancing is a board game full of surprise triumphs and hidden hammer blows. Most weekends I place these accumulator bets on the football. They tend to lose. Small stake, big win, unlikely to triumph, jackpot if they do type thing. I select a number of games and decide whether the home team will win, the away team will triumph or whether the fixture will end in a drawn match. You can pick up to 16 games on one bet and you have to get them all correct, but obviously the odds lengthen the more you add. There is always one game that will let you down.

In mid-December, I stumbled into the sketchy bookmakers on the corner of Withington Road, Manchester, with a savage *Guardian* hangover and placed a silly coupon that somehow won me £934 from a £3 stake, saving me from tax shortfall hell. The moral of this idiotic story is; put 30% of *everything* you earn away. Prepare for the worst, instead of having to turn to gambling, prostitution or drug dealing come January. I didn't feel proud, just relieved that the impending HMRC penalty had been called off.

After that, I took on an accountant that Danny Allison had recommended in Preston because I absolutely detest sitting in my office, with half a tree's worth of receipts, adding them up on a calculator every December, only to hit delete by accident and feel like throwing a heavy object through my window.

When you're self-employed, you have to file an annual tax return to HMRC. I filled out my own on one occasion and it was enough. I came home from my studio late one evening to find a pile of letters on the kitchen worktop. One of them was from HMRC. I had started to receive a steady flow of correspondence since registering Ben and Ink Illustration. Most of them were just reminders of various important dates in the tax calendar.

The tax year runs from April to April each year in the UK and I had registered my business after summer, meaning I was not due to file my first return until the following year. This letter informed me that I now owed them a £100 penalty fee for not filing my tax return in time for the January 31st deadline. Ignoring the letter, knowing I was not due to file until the next year, I was shocked when I received a rapid follow-up, using some legal jargon in a mildly threatening tone, only days later. I was perplexed and angry, so I called them up. The person on the phone admitted the mistake was on their part, but told me I still had to call a different number to explain the situation and only then, when I had proven myself innocent, would the fine be wiped.

Many expenses are tax-deductable provided they are for business. Travel, phone bills, office rent, new equipment, lunches out of home and many more items will be chipped off your gross earnings. It all helps make the bill a bit less daunting when it smashes down your door. Those letters warrant their own entrance; the cat should really be coming in through the tax flap.

If you cannot bring yourself to concentrate long enough to read through pages and pages of instructions and baffling numerical/legal terminology, get an accountant. If you look around, you'll find a decent one at an affordable price and they make your life a hell of a lot easier. If you're skint, get out of the city and find one further out. They can be just as good, but significantly cheaper.

It took me three years of deficit scares to learn, but with 30% of everything going into a separate account, it's much easier. In a nutshell, the way it works is: you turn up at your accountants once a year, in my case with a supermarket carrier bag full of envelopes. In 2010, the bag was from Lidl, 2011 it was Aldi, in 2012, Sainsbury's and in 2013 I bowled in with a Co-operative bag-for-life. They joked that next time it'll be Waitrose.

I keep one envelope for each month's expense receipts and an envelope that contains all my tax year invoices. They answer any questions you might have along the way and make the odd phone call to check you haven't forgotten anything that can be claimed against your bill. Even their fee is tax deductable so it really is win/win. When I received my summary in the post, there were things claimed for I had not even been aware that I could include. The accountant pays for their fee and then some with the money they saved me.

- Once you're in the arts, there are infinite possibilities for moving sideways into other disciplines, through collaboration, networking and hard work.

- Stick to your strengths, applying your key skills to other disciplines is great, but trying to do everything yourself will leave you divided and directionless if you're not careful.

- Different identities or pseudonyms can establish you in other disciplines without diluting your specialist reputation.

- Find a way into places others believe you're not yet ready to be. If you act like you belong and can back it up in performance, people do not question your presence. Be cheeky, do what you have to do to make contacts and inroads.

- Check who someone is before offering them a biscuit and a cup of tea.

- If you know you can do something well and want to earn the chance, do what it takes to prove it. Be robust and inform people you're the top dog. Stretching the truth isn't lying, its just creative compensation to cover your lack of experience.

- When you have a website, you don't know who is watching. Keep portfolios updated and fresh. Don't be afraid to show off (with a dash of modesty).

- Those less experienced teach you things too. Never stop listening and learning, arrogance is fatal.

- Freelance sick days do not exist.

- Educate potential clients. Do not assume people have the vision to apply your existing work to their product. Send them samples, in context, and leave nothing to chance.

- Your portfolio is your shop window, speculate and fine-tune your work to appeal to the audience you want to attract. Broaden your subject matter to expand your potential audience.

- Find an affordable accountant, your time is better spent elsewhere and they will pay for themselves from the money you'll save.

DANNY ALLISON: PHOTOGRAPHER AND ILLUSTRATOR, *TIME* MAGAZINE, BUDWEISER, BBC, EMI RECORDS.

'My brain works very fast. Hyperactive almost. I've often described it as being like a Filofax in the wind. That's what it feels like when I am trying to think about anything. In my illustration, it's all quite fast and explosive. It's almost like I want it to be moving. When you look at the images, they're all over the shop. I think I'm expressing how my brain works to a degree. You don't really choose how your work looks, it's heavily influenced by a personality.'

CHAPTER 10. Mobile Freelancing

How I came to live in New Zealand was the culmination of a strange sequence of events that involved a girl... obviously.

Just as you make plans, things change. I was happy, really happy, in Manchester. One rainy November Monday afternoon, I had taken a walk into town. I was a bit fed up, winter Monday blues, blown out of proportion by shitty weather. Sluggish days are inevitable when you police yourself as a freelancer. So I thought I'd attempt a bit of early Christmas shopping in an effort to salvage something from the day.

Failing almost instantly, I found myself staring into space in a coffee shop as people rushed by with umbrellas and kids struggled to keep up with parents under streetlight. When my second coffee was finished, I set off home and just around the first corner, I was stopped by one of those charity people with the clipboards, who pull you up in the street. My head was all over the place, so I stood there, eyes glazed over on Market Street. As the girl talked, I gradually started to notice that she was quite pretty. As she continued to tell me about 'Crisis,' a young homeless people's charity, I signed up and as I penned the form, I started to think I should ask her out on a date.

My logic was, I couldn't lose. If she said 'yes', I would have a date with a pretty lady, if she said 'no', I would never have to see her again and I would have a comedy tale for Skerritt who I knew would be close by, en route to his shift at Odeon Cinema. She said yes and I met her in Ashton, just outside Manchester on the Friday. It went well, but she travelled all over the country doing this job, which made it logistically unlikely we could have a relationship.

I grew to like the girl and we dated for a few months. After a while, she told me that she had to move back to New Zealand when her VISA ran out. I couldn't shake the idea that this was maybe not a doomed relationship. I had wanted to go to New Zealand since my obsession with *The Lord Of The Rings* movies, which were filmed there. Danny Allison's travels in Australia had made me feel like the toad that lived in the well and only ever saw part of the sky. I needed to get out of it for a while and explore and now seemed like an opportune time to do it, given that I was not tied to one place by my work. I called Danny in Australia and his suggestion that I should not hesitate sealed the deal.

When I look back now, it was a *wild* decision. Upon hearing the news of my emigration, the look on my friends' faces was one of disbelief. I assured Skerritt that I would continue to hold up my side of the Quenched Unsigned project and that I would be available at all times over Skype. He was disappointed but must have seen that I needed to do this and his girlfriend at the time agreed to take my place in the flat.

As far as I was concerned, I was never coming back. I laugh out loud when I think about that now. I had not even skimmed the surface in Manchester and my career was going from strength-to-strength in the UK. Yet here was a valid reason to go to the other side of the world and I worried that, without a reason, I may never do it.

My clients were great. I told them I was going to be travelling for a while, but my work situation would remain the same. They pointed out the fact that I was already working from a different end of the country to them so it was fine, I could keep my monthly slots.

Predictably enough, I spent the first month feeling pretty homesick and the relationship with the girl I'd chased to the other side of the world didn't work at all. Workflow and money were not issues, but I had underestimated the support of my network of close friends and the on-demand contact with my small, tight-knit family.

I started out in a tiny town called Pahiatua, with a population of just 2,000 people. Every time you walked down the high street, people would stop and turn their heads and every time I entered a building or opened my mouth, it was like a scene from a Western movie, when a newcomer walks in the saloon and everything stops dead.

I freelanced three or four days a week, not as much as I did in England, but enough to pay my way. I bought a dongle, which meant I had pay-as-you-go mobile internet wherever I was, even in tiny places like Pahiatua.

The big upside to the time difference was the fact that my UK clients would commission me while I was in bed, then by the time they came to work the next day, a full work session had passed for me, meaning they had a work in progress and sometimes even a finished job on their desk.

During the second week, my homesickness got the better of me and I lost my head completely, packing my bags, sitting there waiting for my girlfriend to come home from work, so I could announce I was sick of it and ready to leave. She looked baffled and asked where I planned on going. I had no car and the nearest town with public transport was ten miles away on the other side of a bottomless gorge. I figured I'd pay a stranger to take me far away from here. Who would turn down $200 to drive me to the nearest town, Palmerston North, right? Then I would think about my next move. I had clearly watched too many action movies. What a f**king idiot. I quietly unpacked.

LOSING IT

October got pretty hot. Summer was starting. I would get up in the morning, shower, call a couple of friends on Skype, then get down to work, which was coming in pretty regularly from UK clients. I still worked for Manchester City, *WSC*, *Design Week*, Leeds United, *The Guardian* and others on a monthly basis and surplus bits would trickle in here and there. I near enough worked for three weeks solid while sluggish and feeling sorry for myself, living alone in Palmerston North, seeing out the remainder of the lease on the flat I'd taken on with my girlfriend.

One of the first clients with whom I had been in contact back in 2008 was *Mixmag*, the UK's number one clubbing and DJ magazine. They didn't care about my location and commissioned me to illustrate this four-page feature about a guy who had been to Exit Festival in Serbia and taken far too many drugs. He woke up and found himself strapped to a table in a Serbian psychiatric hospital. He was gagged and bound and they dosed him each time he awoke, sending him back to sleep before he could explain there had been a mistake. In the end, he managed to convince them he wasn't ill, just a victim of gross over-indulgence and they set him free. The piece was tailor-made for the darker side of my work and I channelled everything into it, given my current mindset, creating these twisted images of psychedelic lizard kings and witches about which this guy had hallucinated. To add to the effect, while trying to coax in a neighbour's cat, I ended up with about 10 flies pinging about in the room, off the walls, buzzing angrily as they bounced off my face. I felt like Jack Nicholson in *The Shining*.

Danni Skerritt was making an absolute nuisance of himself, carving out more opportunities for Quenched Unsigned back in the midst of Manchester's music scene. I missed him a lot and was gutted to learn not only that he'd been invited to attend the next Unconvention event, but he was sitting on a discussion panel that included Billy Bragg and Jarvis Cocker. This was quite a turnaround from our first appearance, sneaking around the backstage areas illegally and underlined the benefits of people remembering your face. We'd chat over Skype most days and he found my current psychosis in the flat hilarious. He told me he was spending most nights at gigs in Manchester and Liverpool, getting to know the latest bands on the scene. He was building quite a network. I continued to art direct the posters for 'No Right to be Here' the name with which we had christened our live band night, quite aptly really...

Since I'd been sat on my backside, without spending much money, I used some of my excess funds to commission Charles Williams, a London-based graphic designer/illustrator, and Andy Thomson, an illustrator also from London, to work on the first couple of designs, I understood the value of broadening the styles of artwork we used and I loved bringing in other creatives and steering the direction of their work. It meant that, though I was exiled from the UK, the Quenched portfolio was getting stronger all the time. It also helped me learn on the job how to art direct, a valuable skill to add to my illustration profession, but one I might struggle to further while based in New Zealand.

OUTDOOR OFFICES

After paying off the flat lease, I was sitting on my hands without a plan when I called Danny Allison one afternoon, aware that only a couple of hours' time difference now separated us. He had made his way down the west coast of Australia with Leona in a camper van that he'd customized as a studio, with a fold-down mattress in the back so that he could use it to sleep and work. Danny invited me to stay with him in Sydney, where he lived in a rented house and planned to stay for a few months, with the promise of enough room to work with him at his place. I booked a flight to Sydney and arrived with my two bags.

Danny and his girlfriend were renting a four-bed house in Glebe, a bohemian suburb of Sydney. I instantly liked the place. I felt at ease because I was staying with a close friend and, within a couple of days, we had resumed the madness we had put on hold in Preston. This time we had sun, sand, city perks and a lot of beautiful new wildlife.

Danny had been out drinking a week prior to my arrival and managed to smash up his leg by falling over the gate to the back of the house, while very drunk, and having left his front door key at home. He had to have more surgery on the knee.

By this point, with a clearer head, I had more or less decided that I would return home when I had enjoyed Sydney and explored New Zealand. I still missed everyone and nowhere in this part of the world could provide the creative noise of the UK with which I felt I needed to fill my head in order to progress. I missed small things about home – the way people *enjoy* moaning; the way the terraced streets have a unique look. I already had around 10 project ideas stockpiled, having taken a step back to assess everything.

On the days when I'd cleared my client work, we'd head off to the beach, go fishing under Sydney Harbour bridge or explore the city, Danny hobbling on his crutch. It constantly wowed me that technology permitted this kind of freedom. I'd stare at the mobile internet device and marvel that I was online next to some idyllic blue, remote lake, the same way some people in small towns still point at aeroplanes each time they pass overhead.

I used salvaged textures and local graphics in my work. The nearest photocopy/print shop had recycling bins that I'd raid for cool symbols and icons. The local customs and characters would inform and inspire my creative output from new angles, with fresh ideas, colours, smells and sounds.

After two weeks sleeping on an airbed at Danny's place booked into the hostel five minutes up the road for a month-long stay. We worked in a little outdoor office furnished with the neighbour's cast-off furniture that they would leave outside on the pavement. Mosquito-repellent coils hung from the clothesline and rainbow lorikeets would land around us. It was our own little urban paradise and it was better than dog mess and our old arctic-cold offices any day of the week. The power leads reached the sockets via a huge extension lead and Danny had the internet at his house, as did the hostel, so I didn't have to use my mobile connection.

I was able to operate fully on the road with the following mobile design kit:

- Macbook Pro laptop computer and charger

- Canonscan Lide 200 flatbed scanner and USB connecting lead

- One can of mid-tone colour spray paint (mid-yellow could be digitally altered to just about any colour)

- 2 tracing paper pads (A4)

- A cartridge paper sketchbook (A4)

- A Preston City Council rubber pencil case made from a recycled tyre, full of various ink pens, brushes, fine pens, pencils and a pot of ink

- Mobile internet (Vodafone dongle)

I'd supplement it with odd packets of crayons or pastels where necessary.

I had the pleasure of doing a *Guardian Sport* illustration during the Ashes cricket test series. England smashed the Aussies and I was commissioned to illustrate an editorial piece conceptually on the desperate scenario, mooted by the world's sporting media, that the natives would be wheeling out a retired Shane Warne to try and save the day. The time difference meant that I was halfway through the job in the hostel living room at 1am, Saturday morning. Drunken Aussies would stumble past, recognize 'Warnie,' then proceed to question my respect for their country and the audacity I had to come here and work for the enemy! I felt like some sort of design undercover agent. The Aussies really hated losing at *anything*. I could relate to that and twisted the knife in my own little way.

STICKING TO YOUR GUNS

I wanted to go to the beach and fall asleep on a towel. That was the plan until Danny was shackled by an illustration commission deadline for Australian *Men's Fitness* magazine. So I thought I'd take the afternoon to do a few chores and update my portfolio.

TV channel E4 brought me in to work on the promotion of the new season of *Skins*, for the second consecutive year, which felt pretty good. They'd bought into my style somewhat for the show's younger, cool brand. This time they gave me a creative licence in the direction of the video, the camera pans, crops and timings. I really fancied this art direction thing.

A friend had recently said to me that my portfolio was starting to look like a university portfolio, in the sense that it was comprised of some pretty sought-after clients, such as *The Guardian*, Channel 4 and Manchester City, the kind of gigs you'd choose for your self-initiated briefs at college, even though you don't think they'll ever *actually* happen. It started me thinking that this was not the result of luck, more perseverance, hard work and a learned self-belief. Although it feels, for much of the time, that you're stumbling along without any kind of direction, with hindsight I could start to see patterns and traceable long-term methods used to attain clients. The foundations had been laid many years before I consciously started professional image-making. All those early drawings of footballers had been declarations of what I had to offer to the creative direction of the sporting world.

Back at university, I was told by one of my tutors that I should prepare to hate the majority of my work; 95% would not be much fun, 3% of it would be all right and only 1% or 2% would be enjoyable. I found this viewpoint a little off-putting.

By this point, two years into full-time freelancing, I would estimate that 90% of my work had become very enjoyable indeed. Some of the earlier jobs I took on were quite dull affairs. They were corporate gigs, focusing mainly on people in suits, reaching for briefcases hanging out of trees, stood on ladders, among other jaded concepts. They paid well enough and there was a temptation to chase more of it by loading my portfolio with them to make fast money. But I never did. I was always glad to see the back of them and doing this kind of work was not why I had buried myself under £15,000 of student debt. I think it comes down to how much you're prepared to sacrifice financially in order to bide your time, make your mark with a style you love as opposed to widening the appeal, diluting and making more money, perhaps at the cost of job satisfaction.

GOOD PRESS

Danni Skerritt was running Quenched Unsigned while I worked with Charles Williams remotely to create the company's new brand and logo. When we had our fresh new look, I started to pester certain areas of the design press about the work we were doing in the music industry, since we had a foot in both art and music camps, I figured someone might want to offer us some form of coverage. Through my work for *Design Week*, the magazine's art director, Sam Freeman, had provided me with the right contact at the magazine who saw something interesting in what Quenched was doing. At best, I had hoped for a side column or a little mention in the corner of the back few pages, if anything, but they ran a four-page lead feature about designers working in the music industry. Not only did they place my work alongside the Sir Peter Blake design for the cover of Sergeant Pepper's *Lonely Hearts Club Band* album, they also ran my Don Letts portrait as front cover of the issue!

After my time in Sydney, I returned, re-energized, to New Zealand. I travelled around in the car I had bought. I made a friend who really helped me out by looking after the car while I was gone. My free roaming, turning around jobs on deserted beaches, on hostel bunk beds and from the look-out point above the nesting habitat of the yellow-eyed penguin, was liberating and full-on adventure. The balance of work and adventure was perfect. I met another illustrator in Nelson who was working remotely too. Was there this whole underground network of us, doing whatever the hell we liked in all corners of the globe?

Before I left for the UK, Danny Allison and his girlfriend joined me in New Zealand so we embarked upon a camping tour of the North Island. It was the first full rest from work I'd taken since I started full-time, two years earlier. During these breaks, you see how easy it is to overkill something you love doing. The time you take off from freelance work is just as crucial as the time you put in. It is surprising just how quickly you fill your head with fresh ideas if you step out of your routine for a minute.

- A change of scenery can be really healthy for restoring waning creativity.

- The world is much smaller thanks to technology and it is infinitely possible to work from most places in the world, provided you have an internet connection.

- Mimicking Jason Bourne is no way to deal with a relationship problem.

- Spending all day alone, indoors, in baking heat is not healthy.

- A camper van can also double up as an office or studio.

- A mobile design studio can fit into one bag, style requirements permitting.

- The creative brain and its powerful imagination can create unnecessary problems.

- Take time off. The freelancer's guilt will bite, but you'll come back stronger for a rest.

CHAPTER 11. UK HUSTLE

By the seven-month mark of my travels in New Zealand and Australia, I was more than ready to embrace the hustle and bustle of England once more, something that was essential if I was to develop creatively. I flew back into Heathrow Airport and immediately found a greasy café. After 30 hours in the air, airport queues and waiting rooms, I needed a cup of tea. They give you Styrofoam brews on long flights if you ask them, but nothing can get close to an English one in a mug, so I tracked down a gloriously grimy little place with plastic seats attached to the tables. The weather was predictably miserable, but I was thrilled to be home and had even missed the murky skies.

After a couple of days rest in Yorkshire, filling in the family on everything that had happened, I had to get back to Manchester and immerse myself in the creative scene. I had no plan whatsoever. My old room was still empty (and the wifi password was the same), so I stayed with Danni Skerritt and his girlfriend, but there's only so long you can lodge with a couple.

My regular clients had briefs waiting for me within the first week, which alleviated the pressure and now that Skerritt and I were in the same postcode again, we would be able to think about the direction in which we needed to drive Quenched. We had decided it would become Quenched Music, shedding the previous and poorly thought out 'unsigned' tag to coincide with Charles William's new branding and eliminate the risk that people might think we only worked with unsigned musicians.

VANISHING BUDGETS

Inside the first month, the shit hit the fan. *The Guardian* announced that the budgets were becoming so tight that it unfortunately had to cull some freelancers. I was one of them. Leeds United decided that the monthly magazine would be discontinued, taking a second client down. Chairman Ken Bates was keeping me awake at night by selling our best players, now he was pulling plugs on my career. Manchester City disappeared without warning or notification, which further underlined the fragility and unpredictability of creative freelancing.

Nobody is under obligation to notify you of any change unless a contract is in place. I had started to panic more about my relationship with my agency, Illustration Ltd. Things were far from fruitful while I was away and I felt that surely, before long, they would consider re-thinking my place with them. I was not wrong.

I talked to them on the phone, with the same sort of schoolboy-in-trouble adrenaline pumping through me as when you receive a text from a someone you're head-over-heels in love with saying: 'We need to talk'. They asked if I felt that I could benefit more from a different agency. Was this a push or a genuine, honest question? They were adamant that it was very much the latter, so I explained that I had the Next clothes store murals to upload to my portfolio, along with a bunch of new personal pieces I had created based on Harry's advice. I really felt this would add a new dimension to my style. My feelings were that this might take two or three months to bear fruit and the agency was happy to hear that I had been working hard to turn things around. To their credit, they let me make the call and agreed to take another look at where things stood in three months' time.

I appreciated how friendly, honest and professional Illustration Ltd had been with me. With a year-and-a-half of false starts under my belt, they had every right to drop me. But they didn't. I just prayed I could start to repay their faith.

Just when I thought things couldn't get any worse, I woke to an email from Sam Freeman from *Design Week*. Assuming it was a new commission, I instead learned that the print magazine was to be discontinued with immediate effect: that meant redundancy for Sam and many other members of staff. This was all getting a bit serious. Staring through the tiles behind the kettle, I started to question the wisdom of my decision not to promote myself during my time in New Zealand and Australia. Despite the great adventure I'd had, I was now wondering if I should have pulled the car over and fired off 10 emails to potential clients each day? With four regulars now scythed from under me, things were starting to feel precarious and I could feel the hot breath of employment agencies panting down the back of my neck, anticipating my return through their doors.

On a positive note, the nextdoor neighbours in Manchester came by to say 'hello' and asked if I would be interested in renting their spare room, which was available for a decent price, bills included. I was now only one wall away from being right back where I started.

It felt like those virgin days at Oyston Mill all over again. I found myself dusting off the database and not quite sure where the next rent cheque was coming from. Every day I felt *too* freelance, exposed to the cruel harshness of it all, unsure whether it was evening or morning as days merged into one. I became quite angry for a while; ranting in blog posts, about 'the reality of being a creative' as a form of venting. I was just furiously lashing out through my writing. Now it's plain to see that my blog was the earliest form of this book, but you'd think I'd been falsely imprisoned judging by the venom those words packed.

Strategically staggering my walks to the local grocer, Tesco and bargain centre was one bizarre defence mechanism I developed to fend off the cabin fever. My shaves became a diary event; in the place of social outings that would cost me money, I'd put on the radio, light little candles on the side of the bath and take my time with every glide of the razor. I actually looked forward to them. If I had a fresh blade or facial soothing product featuring 'ice' or 'cool wave' in the title, I might even sneak out for a chocolate bar to mark the extra special occasion. If football commentary was on the radio, some shaves would last upwards of an hour. I found myself making beard art until I ran out of face space. Big side burns with connecting moustache, Hogan handlebars, Chaplin toothbrush, clean-shaven and then bed, little ways to make myself laugh amid the panic.

The bags under my eyes started to feel heavier, my legs felt like snapped candles whenever I left the house, from the lethargy, and my eyes intermittently twitched due to stress. This time, I did not even have the company of Danny Allison, Danni Skerritt or Rich Taylor throughout the day. Luckily for me, my social saving grace was free entry to most gigs in town and our open mic night, Acoustic Broth, which Skerritt was still running. I found myself scouring the options for free entertainment more robustly than ever before. It was now a necessity to make human contact in the evenings at least four days-a-week.

I continued to go to the open mic nights at Gullivers with Skerritt, but things were moving very slowly on the work front and every social outing was underpinned by a pulsating guilt, brought on by the lack of paid employment. Every penny you spend seems to do twice the damage when you're not winning any work. I overheard a conversation between two friends from which I learned that, apparently, it costs you somewhere in the region of 50p to boil the kettle. This didn't help my psyche.

I really struggled to get myself motivated to do anything about the situation. You fall down this black hole and everything gets mixed up, the positives hide and the negatives sit on your face. You're quiet, so you should be marketing. But you're not because morale is low. Instead, you're sweeping the flat or walking to the shop to look at the offers of the week.

When I was studying at university, one illustrator came in to do a talk. Someone asked him about working from home and he detailed how he had secretly become addicted to his son's video games during a quiet spell. He would take his boy to school, then when his wife had left for work, fire up the machine and play the games for hours. On one occasion, she returned unexpectedly at lunchtime and when he heard the key in the lock, he tried to jump up, switch off the machine and make it to his office before she could catch him. He had spent so long sat in an awkward position that his legs did not immediately work properly and he took two lunges, then cascaded down the staircase, landing at her feet with a thud. 'You've been playing the games again, haven't you, dear?' she quizzed him rhetorically as he lay there groaning, belittled.

I found myself looking at the jobs market, more out of feeling sorry for myself than any genuine desire to return to work. This was the first time searching since my peanut butter heartbreak and I went as far as applying for some really silly positions including one job that revolved around making short films about the contents of the stuffed animal collection with teams of students at the Manchester Museum. They never got back to me.

SAVING MONEY

To say I became a total oddball during this personal downturn is putting things mildly. Danni Skerritt and I would go for walks in the evenings or head to a gig. My flatmates were at work or off doing things most evenings so if Skerritt was busy with his girlfriend, I had to amuse myself. I started to walk a lot, just aimless strolls for miles at a time, all around my local area and various routes through the park. I witnessed the outbreak of the Manchester riots while drifting as far as the city centre one afternoon.

One thing I started to get into was visiting all the local supermarkets to see what reduced price food was available.

I found myself in Asda at strange times like 11.30pm and 3pm, trying to find a pattern in the times they put the little yellow 'whoops' stickers on the food that was about to go out of date. I was not alone in doing this.

It didn't matter what time you went to the Co-op on Withington Road, there was some other chancer sniffing around the employee holding the price sticker gun, ready to snatch at their trolley before the packet even touched the shelf. If you tried to slip into the Tesco on Upper Chorlton Road, unnoticed, at 2.30pm, you would be caught out by the mother who had set off too early to collect her kid from the nearby primary school and had just nipped in to 'kill ten minutes' beating me to the Ginsters chicken and mushroom slice, now 28p, down from £1.49. It didn't take long to learn that you must never underestimate the old ladies. That vulnerable innocence they portray; it's a ruse and they will snatch your blackberry tart if you even think about putting it down for a moment. They are not above using physicality to get what they need.

I found myself getting really upset when there was nothing good on the shelves, so I'd stretch my legs by marching around all of my local areas, bargain hunting. It became something you just wanted to be a part of, like a little social club, rather than actually wanting or needing anything. Transit friendships occasionally blossomed there.

Skerritt, it turned out, had been doing this for months while I had been behaving like a human being in New Zealand, as opposed to the freelance dog I had become since returning. Just when I had started to get an idea of the timetable, he took me on a crash course. The closest one, Tesco, on

Withington Road was ripe for the picking at 4.30pm until 5.30pm. You might get lucky at other times, but as a rule, this was the opportune time to pounce, he told me. On one occasion, we each came away with pork loin, chicken breast and three loaves of bread for under £3 and spent the next 24 hours feasting like kings. Co-op's prime time was an hour later and Asda was only half an hour later than the Tesco. It really depended on where you were at the time. I was not beneath running from one to the other in order to catch both, if I was really up for it.

Skerritt told me that, on one occasion, he'd seen a fight break out at the reduced chiller section in Asda. A couple had been juggling a few items, not having fetched a trolley. When they momentarily put down their goods, the vulture next to them reached over and lifted their steaks. The wife demanded the return of the steaks, but the vulture argued they were now his as they had 'touched the shelf'. The husband was obliged to diffuse the situation, which was becoming heated. The vulture refused to return the steaks and the wife began shouting and swearing. Just when everyone's focus was on the three people in conflict, a man standing next to Skerritt kicked down a pyramid of bean tins, laughing and fleeing the scene. The original three then had to be separated by security.

I eventually cut my visits down to the times when I was passing for another reason or actually *needed* something. I was out of control in the depths of this work slump, unable to think clearly or behave rationally.

BEWARE THE INTERNET

Freelancers probably spend more time online than most. On one occasion, I worked really late, updating websites and creating new portfolio illustrations. It was raining torrentially outside and I didn't want to leave the flat to buy food. With four eggs left in the cupboard, which were six days past their sell-by date, I was unsure whether I should eat them. My flatmates were out somewhere and Skerritt's lights were off nextdoor. He knows about sell-by dates for some reason, but I dare not chance waking him, So I Googled the matter.

I found this site called 'Mumsnet' where mothers congregate online and share secret mum things. I found myself agreeing or disagreeing with them, siding with someone over an argument about whether the punishment for Janet's teenage son's smuggling of a girl into his room was justified. I didn't comment, (you had to sign up to do that) but I was really getting into the thread. The setting up of a fake account crossed my mind, maybe a disguise as 'Paula' or 'Dianne' would be more convincing than 'Marilyn' or 'Epiphany.' I spent about 45 minutes following the debate before eventually returning to the eggs thread. It turned out that Sandra, from Chester, was in the same predicament, but she had her man putting her under pressure to go out and buy new ones. The general consensus was that he was being a dick. I departed the conversation at:

'Thank you, however he's refusing to eat them anyway. So I'm going to use them up in a cake or something. I was just annoyed that they were going to be wasted. In other news, we just had our first fight.' *Sandra, Chester.*

I cracked my out-of-date eggs onto a white sheet of brand new 150gsm paper as per the advice in the thread. They looked fine, it was not salmonella that would prove my undoing, but something far more innocent-seeming. It's always the things you least suspect... The next morning, I was distracted by a few crumbs on the living room floor while making a cup of tea. Grabbing the broom to sweep them up (rather than emailing the people who could give me work, as I should have been doing) I caught the Ethernet cable connecting to my flatmate's PC desktop and dragged down the wireless router. It smashed onto the floor with an ominous cracking noise.

I dropped the brush and slid on my knees like a kid at a wedding, grabbing the device, all in one motion, knowing what had happened before I even looked. To my horror, the bit that goes in the back port and supplies power had cracked and we only owned one. This meant *the internet was down*, possibly the worst thing that could happen to a freelancer. The lady on the phone at Talk Talk took me through many processes, but none of them was any good without a new adaptor, which could only be with us in five-to-seven working days.

I sat there, breathing heavily on the sofa, the only other sound was the footsteps of the toddler running about in the flat above. The pathetic irony was not lost on me; as a five-year-old's life blossomed upstairs, a 28-year-old's was grinding to a halt, like some kind of severed root.

In the midst of my delirious self-loathing, I picked up the phone and called the guys at my old studio. In under an hour, I had rejoined Openspace. I figured it would be better to break the bank than hand over my mind. I felt anxious, confused and angry that I had come this far, at 28 years of age, with three years' freelancing experience, only to crumple into a wreckage of my former self. I felt somewhat wronged to be back in my overdraft and all-but-unemployed again, the reset button held firmly down.

- Workflows change fast and not always for the better. Keep promoting yourself, even when you're stupidly busy.

- One of the keys to longevity is to consolidate success when you're winning.

- The right agency will stand by you and be patient, provided you meet them halfway and work hard to improve things.

- Shaving should not be a diary event, try to get out often if you work from home, cabin fever is counter-productive.

- Reduced price food items are great, but should not consume any more time than a passing visit.

- The internet can be a huge distraction. Misspent time adds up, be strict with yourself.

- In a negative mindset, it is easy to lose perspective. You are not awful, just going through a rough patch. So are many other people.

- Negotiation is a fine art, there is always a little room in either direction.

- Save your chores until after work, even if you work at home.

SAM PRICE: FREELANCE ART DIRECTOR, *TOP GEAR* MAGAZINE, *MATCH OF THE DAY* MAGAZINE, *Q* MAGAZINE, *BIG ISSUE* (ART DIRECTOR 2007-2011)

'There are a lot of journeymen, one bloke is a really good veteran designer, he's spitting blood; worse off now than ten years ago. The problem is, the big brands see the mass of designers, photographers, illustrators and they say, 'Well, take it or leave it.' Someone will do it. If I quit my slot tomorrow, three or four people would come in on the same day rate and that's not nice to know. Thankfully, there's always the number one illustrator or artist and people still pay for quality. But what happens when number one knocks you back, then two, three. Before you know it you're scratching around at degree shows. It all comes down to disposable budget.'

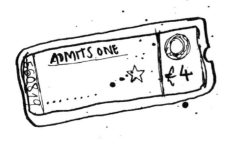

CHAPTER 12. BUDGET TRAVEL

Jeff Thomson, a director of Manchester music initiative 'Unconvention' told me that Megabus has been the reason the independent music industry has survived for the past 10 years. He was only half joking. I had boarded one or two of these budget coach services between Preston and London in my time, but had to reacquaint myself with them, given the absence of paid work. Virgin Trains had upped their fares again, leaving me with no alternative but to bite down on the leather and take the pain of the five-hour ride. It's a total lottery whether you'll get a double seat to yourself and a functioning plug socket, or a heaving beast next to you, emitting seven strains of body odour. Heaven forbid you take a hangover on a Megabus.

I visited London semi-regularly by this point, both to visit work targets with my portfolio and to teach at Central Saint Martins. If I wanted either venture to be cost-effective, Megabus was the only option with fares advertised as starting from £1 each way between Manchester and London. Just don't use the toilet.

Reading more books in the evenings was one positive to emerge during this testing work drought. In George Orwell's *Down and Out In Paris and London,* where the writer lives rough in the French capital while pursuing his writing ambitions, he learned a tactic of licking garlic, since its strong taste would last for hours, fooling his brain into believing the body had been fed recently, among other little tricks. It occurred to me that I'd subconsciously developed many little tactics of my own that would save me money during leaner spells.

Taking an empty cup from another table in a coffee shop and pretending to take a last sip from it just as the staff came to clear the table, before thanking them kindly as they take it away, was one. It meant you didn't have to buy a drink to sit in the café; though some of them clearly knew I hadn't bought one, thanks to computer systems logging table transactions, and that was embarrassing. Vaulting train barriers was an obvious, but occasionally effective, money-saver, one that had to be saved for *really* dark days. Avoiding the ticket stamp is a classic. I knew one guy who would write make an 'out of order' sign with a marker pen and an A4 sheet of paper, tape it to the train toilet door, then sit and read for the duration. It worked, though on one occasion it resulted in a police chase through London Euston train station.

Never, under any circumstances, pay to use a public toilet. Crawl under the turnstile if you have to. If you pull the metal bar backwards a little, there is just enough room to shuffle through. A nice smile or a fake phone conversation is sufficient to throw staff at McDonald's and other fast food chains if you don't feel confident enough to sneak into their facilities. I could go on... None of us wants to stoop to these tactics, but it's Darwinian out there at times.

BACK ON THE HORSE

Doing my best to prevent the rising apathy from throttling me completely, I started to force myself to concentrate sufficiently to create new works on topics upon which I had not yet touched in my portfolio. Cars, Dobermans and gadgets, images that could work in fashion marketing and design all busied me for a while. Then I had a go at science; space after that. Sometimes a blank canvas and a whole galaxy of subject matter can be more frightening than a tightly prescribed brief.

It's too easy to fall into the trap of looking at what other creatives are up to. You only notice how cut-throat the level of talented competition in the arts is when things look bleak. It's a total professional warzone and someone is always turning up with a seemingly more devastating weapon. By creating specific pieces with a targeted client in mind, I had at least found a way to use the free time positively.

The hope is that the hand-drawn microbes and neurological textures you have prepared, in order to show how you'd illustrate science topics, will be exactly where the art director of the science monthly's eyes settle after their mid-afternoon coffee and cigarette break. If you're lucky, a lunchtime pint or three might help your cause. A lot of people in the arts love a beer at lunchtime and everyone knows daytime drinking affects you faster. If they sidle back into the office, feeling all tank-proof, there's a reasonable chance the alcohol forcefield may numb any risk they might have earlier attached to commissioning you, just one of many completely unpredictable factors affecting your chances of gaining commissions.

Pressing 'send', you watch your URL portfolio travel many cyber miles and cross your fingers, willing it to collide with the mass of atoms representing the junior designer's eyes as they search for a fast solution to the lack of suitable stock photographs for the opinion piece on page 28.

You have to use all your self-belief to trust that somehow, (A) the time it took for the kettle to boil to make coffee at said magazine's cafeteria area, multiplied by (B) the slight delay in copy arriving from the writer of said column, equals something in the ball park of (C) the time you chose to send your link. Even if it does, the tone of language you employed in your email introduction had better be right. It's complete chance and circumstance out there.

There is a degree of science in certain areas of work-seeking. They say 2pm on a Tuesday is the optimum approach time; 11am on Fridays is great too. It's been suggested that there are key times in the week when most people in full-time roles are more susceptible to marketing tactics. It might be time to wind down before the weekend, therefore the client may be feeling relaxed, even chirpy, on a Friday, but for heaven's sake, don't wait too late. Once their mind is in the pub or on the sofa, they won't bother to lift a finger, let alone get back to you. On Tuesday, after lunch, people have just about put the pieces back together after the weekend and can probably spare two minutes to skim through your portfolio.

If your website takes 13 seconds to load compared with the 18-second load time of the guy-across-town's site, even if it is thanks to their overstretched communal internet, you're already five seconds (and less irritation for the art director) ahead of your rival. Just watch the way most Londoners react to seeing that the next underground train is more than one minute away…You just have to pick your moment and hope it's the right one to pounce.

A lack of response never means that you're being ignored. It doesn't mean that they dislike you either, it just exemplifies how busy people are, especially now, with fewer and fewer staff. But when you're in the angry or self-pity headspace I found myself in, everyone is a raging a***hole until you put the kettle on. Only with a cup of tea in hand are you welcomed back to reality and the understanding that this is the nature of the beast, not a personal attack on you.

PLATE SPINNING

In late summer 2011, Danni Skerritt and his girlfriend parted ways and, in a matter of weeks, I was moving my things from next-door, straight back to my old bedroom. My re-hired studio proved financially unsustainable since losing all my regular work and my second stint there didn't last long. The cabin fever returned, but this time, with Skerritt working from home too, I had someone to take down the rabbit hole with me.

Getting dressed in the mornings was becoming an endangered ritual. But in the strange way freelancing seems to catch you off guard, two jobs came my way in one week. My tail was up, especially as one was a return of *The Guardian*, my first outing with the newspaper in months, this time in the education section. The other job came from the newly launched Hamburg branch of Illustration Ltd, for Nissan's company magazine. They'd seen my new car illustrations, the fruits of free time, and brought me in to illustrate a feature. It wasn't the mortgage-sealer I'd been craving, but it was a suggestion that things might improve and some interesting plot twists soon followed.

Just before I'd headed off to New Zealand, I had been brought in to work on a DVD sleeve design for a local indie filmmaker, Mark Ashmore, by a mutual friend. *The Lost Generation* was Mark's current project and debut feature film and he wanted me to design the poster, but had no budget. I didn't feel it was a worthwhile voluntary job. Instead of rejecting it immediately, I thought about what else I could gain from his experience in the film industry. I told him about my work with Quenched Music and that art direction for screen appealed to me, but that kind of work was hard to find without the industry contacts or prior experience. It turned out that, in order to make the film, he had acquired a micro-budget by way of a bank loan and a generous grandparent. This would merely cover actors' fees and post-production suite hire, so if I wanted the role of art-director, it was mine for the taking on a voluntary basis, including the movie poster design, something I had not yet had the opportunity to work on. We both hung up our phones feeling pretty happy.

Freelancers are vague when it comes to talking about money. If a job looks good in the portfolio and is worth doing, nobody needs to know whether it was voluntary or big money. I developed a set of suitably vague template answers, to protect me from disclosing figures, on which I could fall back whenever anyone asked me about my earnings. That way, to the untrained eye, the self-initiated work could be classed as just as impressive as any of the lucrative commissions, if they were sufficiently well-presented.

'It's not too bad, it pays the bills.'

'I can't complain, really.'

'Could be better but you have to think about the long game.'

'They pay all right, but it'll go straight into the void.'

In Danny Allison's absence, I commissioned a local photographer to take promo shots of Skerritt and me for the Quenched website, using the Nissan fee to pay for it. One thing I knew I had to maintain during this slippery patch was ongoing investment (the little I could spare) back into my work, if I was to break out of the slump. It was an ordeal every time I relinquished a pound, but I knew there was no way around that and had to force myself to believe that all was not lost.

The photo shoot was no ego exercise. Skerritt had become such a friendly face on the Manchester music scene that someone recognized him in almost every pub we walked into and I wanted to capitalize on that. We wanted to run with the personal touch that had started to characterize Quenched and I felt that if people saw our faces as part of the brand, it would do just that. We wanted people to feel a part of what we were trying to build.

To create a low-budget, but effective, set design for our shoot, I painted type and naive inky images on £3 rolls of lining paper from hardware stores and hung them behind us on the walls of the Black Lion pub basement, which Mark Ashmore had taken over as his new creative base. He gave us open access to the whole building, since I had helped him out for free on *The Lost Generation* so we had our shoot location. It was wonderfully dingy down there and it worked with the artwork style. He didn't care if we messed up the walls from time-to-time. You can pick up overhead projectors pretty cheaply from eBay, £66 in my case. I printed Skerritt's journal notes and my doodles on acetate, then beamed it onto the two of us and knocked out the main lights.

Skerritt was also effectively out of work at this point. He'd poured a one-litre cup of Pepsi, complete with ice cubes, over a colleague's head, in front of a huge queue of customers at Odeon, after he'd taken exception to patronizing backchat. He quit that job in the same state of mind in which I had left Waterstones; not loathing the job, but craving the pursuit of his freelance career. Now signing on the dole, he was voluntarily sound engineering at Gullivers, picking up new skills and valuable contacts.

Soup Kitchen, one of the venues at which we reviewed gigs, had some decent DJ decks. The manager told Skerritt that if he wanted to come down in the afternoons, mid-week, to practice, that would be fine, after he expressed a need to try his hand following a drunken claim that he could easily DJ better than some of the existing talent.

In the daytime, there's a whole different world beneath the club-and-pub scene. All these shadow people with good contacts and better equipment. If you can convince them to let you into their world, something at which Skerritt was a master, they are useful people to know. Bars and clubs double as great exhibition spaces and locations for talks too.

Skerritt had signed up to the Apple Store's tuition of 'Logic,' the industry-standard programme for making beats and composing music, and wanted to try DJing on actual decks. He spent a lot of time in Soup Kitchen, getting to grips with the basics and playing to a room full of ghosts, while the staff upstairs prepared the venue for the evening's opening. His seemingly endless ability to open locked doors to new opportunities over a pint was beautiful to watch in motion.

It became a bit of a game, wondering how many different areas of the arts we could lever ourselves into. We may have been self-unemployed, but we were excited about getting up in the mornings again. Our friendship really saw us through the lean days in the flat. We always kept the faith that by planting these seeds and trying to remain upbeat, when paid work came again, we'd be much better equipped for the future.

♦ ROGER BROWNING: DESIGN DIRECTOR, *THE GUARDIAN* NEWSPAPER, 1995-2013

'Creatively, it's difficult. We derive enormous enjoyment from commissioning illustration. Every week, in a sense, we used to negotiate with one another. If you're going to commission illustrations for four or five different sections, you've got to be careful they don't look too similar. They need to be utterly different. There was that discussion between us - who would we get to do different things? Then there's the relationship with the illustrator when you're art directing them to do the covers. I really miss that. It happens so rarely now.

Sarah (Habershon, art director) does still commission for her sections occasionally, but not that often. Most often we're having to make do with resources within the building, getting people to do retouching or coming up with things ourselves. The problem that creates is finding the time to do it ourselves. At the same time that our budget has shrunk, the department has downsized too. So there are fewer designers working on the paper. The consequence is that all our workloads have increased. The problem of having to do what we might have farmed out to the *freelance illustrator is that that's more of our time and it's more pressure. It becomes problematic.*

The way photography works, you pay an annual fee. Then you can basically use any pictures that they send for free. It's not free – but a fraction of the overall subscription, so you know where you are. It means that the cost of using a photograph is a fraction of what it costs to use an illustration. The crux of the problem is that, actually, if you look at the cost of each column to produce, illustration, although the fees are not huge, is still one of the most expensive ways of filling a page. Particularly if you're using an agency image, you're spending maybe at most 10% of what you would spend to commission an illustration, but probably not even that. We do still commission photographers to do portraits and other stuff for us. Most often, they're our own photographers or people under contract to us. It's a saving, but it's not good for illustration.

I think that the newspaper isn't as visually interesting because of the lack of variation and that's… that's quite painful for me because, in the past, The Guardian has had a great reputation for its use of illustration. I feel that we've almost lost that now. In the places where we do still use it, in the columns and the comments pages, we do make a real effort to make sure we've got good, interesting people doing the stuff, so I do hope people still look upon us as a kind of high bar in our use of illustration.'

FAILED VENTURES

Although we joked about seeing how far we could go in terms of muscling into new sectors of the arts, not everything paid off. Among all these exciting side projects lay a hidden snake that Skerritt and I named 'Deck Fool.' I wanted to try my hand at live art and pitched an idea to him that involved me painting the banners live, while he played his DJ set. We managed to get a booking on a Thursday night at AXM Manchester, a gay club on Princess Street.

By the time we rolled up with a backpack full of huge rolls of lining paper, Sellotape™, pens and paints, with a 6' wood board, in case the paper wouldn't stick to their surfaces and Skerritt's decks, we realized they'd sacked the guy who booked us and he had neglected to tell the new staff about tonight's event. So we swaggered into the empty club, wearing matching T-shirts designed and printed especially for the occasion, straight past the new management and covered the DJ booth in paper, spraying paints and splashing inks all over the place. It took twenty minutes for one of the junior staff members to be sent over to ask who we were and what the hell we were doing. We tried to explain but the music was so loud that he couldn't hear a word we were saying. The poor guy just looked more befuddled. No punters arrived and, at 11pm, we packed up and left, to the utter confusion of the staff. We consigned Deck Fool to the 'at least we found out' bin.

CAFÉ CULTURE

Coffee shops and cafés became little weekday refuges to offset the increasingly volatile practice of working from home. My laptop battery would last about four hours, so I'd either head into town with my sandwich and find a place with wireless internet and settle in a corner for the afternoon, or get straight out in the morning and return early afternoon. One of my old flatmates worked at Starbucks and would come home with these tales of middle-class anarchy and I was getting to witness these scenes first-hand from behind the shelter of my laptop screen.

I started to find the places a source of amusement while I worked quietly in the corner. People would come in for work meetings and adopt a rude attitude just to impress clients. I saw a woman demand that the staff stopped everything they were doing, including making drinks for fellow customers, and start her coffee again, just because they had stirred it anti-clockwise. Occasionally, you'd get student couples with big folders and A4 notepads passionately kissing in front of you without a hint of shame. I threw rolled up sugar sachets at them if they ever took it too far. Get back to your halls!

Then there were the babies. Whether you're on the Megabus or on caffeine, there are always the wailing babies. The mothers must have been sick of irritating kids' TV presenters, so they bring them in for babyccinos and chai-latte.

If I wanted a change, I had a good selection of caffeine dens in Manchester. The Greggs bakery on Oxford Road had recently installed window seats and, though its coffee was rubbish, it was cheaper than that of the swankier Café Nero up the road. If I was on a morning café shift, I'd buy a coffee and a croissant from Greggs and then log onto the Café Nero wireless internet which you could just about pick up from the right-hand corner, on the bench in the window. Greasy spoon cafés like Antonio's, near Manchester's Piccadilly station, were great if I just wanted a change of scene and an escape from internet distractions.

Freedom to roll around on buses and roam the city on foot was great to a point, but the café-dwelling was only delaying what was starting to feel like the inevitable. It felt like time was passing me by and work had dried up really badly aside from the renaissance with *The Guardian* and my one-job stand with Nissan's magazine. I had applied and failed to land a part-time, three days-per-week lecturing role at UCLAN, my old university in Preston. I scoured the job market and found it quite a morale-burying experience. I either lacked the digital skills or the qualifications for design roles and there are no illustration positions of employment, as such. You can't get much more freelance than illustration, unless you're an astronaut. I had given it everything, lived some dreams, but sadly, it felt like it would soon be over. I didn't even bother to see what level I had slipped to on my wrestler league table, instead I wondered if the recruitment agency I had once worked for still had my CV.

VICTORIA PEARCE: FORMER FASHION AND PHOTOGRAPHY AGENT, CURRENT AGENT AT ILLUSTRATION LTD

'On average, 400 illustrators per week submit their work to Illustration Ltd, seeking representation. Obviously we cannot take on everybody. We go through all of the submissions and we actively seek new talent at exhibitions, degree shows, on blogs etc. Then every quarter, we submit a shortlist at our new talent meetings. It's tough, but we whittle it down to nine or so candidates. We look for an exceptional quality of work, interesting techniques and unique qualities. The truth is, gut feeling plays a huge part. We don't often know what we're looking for until we see it.'

NETWORKING

Creative networking events are full of people who'd rather be somewhere else, proffering business cards, who are waiting for someone else to make the first move and speak. It's a bit like a school disco. You usually take a friend along to make it a bit easier, but even then, instead of trying to identify the 'popular kids', there's a lot of staring, attempting to deduce who looks sufficiently important to give you work. There's always someone who looks stereotypically professional, in an expensive suit with really nice business cards on uncoated stock and embossed gold-leaf type, but lets you down by revealing they work for Barclays bank in Preston and they're just here with a friend. There's the friend of a colleague who you've already met and with whom you've had a long conversation, but you were too drunk on free Chardonnay at the time to remember their face or name now. You can tell those ones straight away, they look at you like you're fresh dog mess on the bottom of their shoe when you say it's nice to meet them. It's better to go with 'nice to see you'. The risk of another tiny humiliation is then erased.

I'd gone alone to an event at The Cornerhouse that I had seen advertised a few days earlier, during one of my coffee shop outings. This event was quite busy and there were a couple of people I knew there. One of them was Mark Ashmore, there to promote *The Lost Generation* film, so we talked about a few new ideas for the project and he introduced me to Rupert Cade, a guy who ran a digital media company in town. I said I'd come by his office and show him my work sometime.

I visited him a week later and, after meeting his staff and introducing them to my portfolio, we discussed potential work opportunities. He mentioned on the way out that if I were ever in town and needed a space in which to work, I should give him a shout. The offer was an attractive one and I couldn't get back to my room quickly enough to email him to follow up. My assumption that a city centre office would cost a lot was probably accurate, but Rupert kindly chose not to charge me a penny if I agreed to help them out with the odd illustration or concept sketch. I didn't think twice, we had a deal.

I used that desk a lot and it put in me in a much better mindset. I set up at the back of the room and kept myself to myself, but the crucial feeling of arriving at work was back and I started to send off emails seeking commissions instead of feeling sorry for myself in my bedroom or staring into space in coffee shops.

Naturally, I muscled in on the hot drinks rota. It was a quiet place in a sort of attic/loft-type office. The place had a pool table and some comfy sofas with a projector for critique sessions and presentations. Without much to work on, I sketched set design ideas for *The Lost Generation* and developed personal work amongst the promo emailing and phone calls.

One afternoon, right before I was about to leave to go and lie on my sofa for a weekend of worrying, the Hamburg office of my Illustration agency got in touch. They had been approached for an urgent job, a marketing campaign for Lufthansa Airways.

I did a little digging and quickly learned that Lufthansa was a fairly big airline and they had a long-standing and respected design reputation. They pushed the boat out in their campaigns and had a whole back-catalogue of original, great looking visuals. Remarkably, within the hour, the job was 100% confirmed. Lufthansa had chosen four illustrators and artists with edgy, 'street art' styles and wanted us each to create artworks of 15 of their flight destinations in our own styles. They would then create a giant mural in the centre of Berlin, a kind of installation piece, before they rolled it out worldwide in the new campaign. The problem was, they wanted it finished by Tuesday morning. How can you prepare the mind for such extremes? For lethargy to be blown away by intense pressure in a matter of minutes?

Things can turn around just like that. In the space of one hour, a job that would take four days of work and pay me enough money to live on for the next three months had fallen into my lap. It's strange how these things seem to cross your path when you're thinking positively. I think the negative headspace causes you to be too introspective and miss opportunities that are in front of you.

In the music industry, they say it takes 10 years to become an overnight success and it's so true. It is a business where everyone is late, phones are rarely answered and everything is subject to change. Bands that 'burst onto the scene' have endured more rejection than people could ever know. It's the same across all of the arts. Over my many barren months, the stress had not been wasted energy; I had been saved by an airline and this one felt as good as any previous triumphs.

- Keeping your head down during quiet spells and broadening your portfolio can bring long-term rewards, even if it all feels bleak, and it makes it easier to sleep at night.

- Timing is crucial when marketing. Try to consider the times and days you choose for contacting people, consider the client's possible schedule and mindset before approaching.

- Self-belief comes with experience and there will always be days of self-doubt. Ride them out, they come and go.

- Learning 'on the job' in new areas can be fun and can bring a greater creative freedom, but make sure you assess the long-term value before accepting any voluntary work.

- Never tell people you did something for free. They don't need to know and the CV entry is just as valid regardless of payment.

- Stay alert to opportunities. You never know what might come from an awkward conversation in a bar.

- You don't always need a qualification to do something different with your skills. Desire and willingness to work hard and learn go just as far.

- Coffee shops and cafés are great surrogate offices if you can work remotely. They help keep the madness at bay when working from home.

- You can often pick up a expensive café's free wifi from a few doors down if you buy a drink in the cheaper one and log in from there. Test it from outside the shop before committing to buying a drink.

- Things can change overnight, never quit, even if you need to go back to work for a short while and save capital.

 KEN GARLAND, BRITISH GRAPHIC DESIGNER AND AUTHOR OF *'THE FIRST THINGS FIRST MANIFESTO.'*

'Early exponents of related studies (at university) helped me to discover William Blake who has been my godfather in every sense, since I discovered his words, images, poetry. His fusion of words and pictures is, in a sense, what I try to do. How lucky to have been in touch with teachers who showed me new things and pointed me in the right direction.'

CHAPTER 13. Dreams Do Come True

The Lufthansa job changed everything for me, psychologically. I was astounded by how everything turned around so fast. What felt like a never-ending spell of unemployment ended and, in almost biblical fashion, the clouds parted. The earnings for this advertising job had been good and laid foundations for the next few months and, all of a sudden, my past achievements transformed from trophies that would only ever gather dust after everything failed, to valuable assets moving forward. My story so far had been placed in an entirely positive light by this glimmering gem of a job for a German airline. It made the path ahead a little more visible.

With this renewed confidence and resolve, I picked up where I had left off before the slump and once again started to send out my best efforts thus far. I updated my databases, freshened-up my website and begun exploring the world of LinkedIn, which everyone around me had derided as a waste of time. However, during our stay in Sydney, Danny Allison and I had discovered otherwise, if you knew how to use it. It was here, several years earlier, that I had sent out a request to David Hilton, creative director of World Wrestling Entertainment.

One morning, I sent him a portrait of a WWE superstar that I'd been drafting in my free time. Then...

'Ben, nice work, give me a call in a couple of days. Cheers, Dave'.

Sitting on my bed with my mouth open, reading and re-reading the reply, I felt like I might vomit.

The Sin Cara portrait had been crafted in the care-free confidence that follows a decent payday like my Lufthansa commission. It showed. My colour use had come along in leaps and bounds and my drawing was getting better.

When you love something as much as I love professional wrestling, the idea of any form of first-hand encounter with your object of affection seems as impossible as understanding life and death.

I'd nudged Dave Hilton, the creative director of digital and print at WWE several more times and he'd eventually returned my messages, apologizing for his crazy schedule, saying he'd take a look. He didn't get back to me and I had not continued the correspondence after my clients ran for the hills and I fell into a negative slump.

Sporadically updating him over the past few years with both new client work and specific wrestling illustration samples never felt like it was achieving much, but here was a phone call invitation that reminded me of the way Roger Browning's invitation for coffee had delivered eventual results a couple of years earlier. Before this recent boost, I had not truly believed that WWE would consider me for a moment. Now, I felt as if it was worth at least knocking on the door one more time.

I'm a grown man who still keeps his hand-drawn WWE VHS cassette covers in his wardrobe and occasionally straps a replica world heavyweight championship belt around his waist in front of the mirror. I bought that belt from my brother with money earned during my 2009 purple patch, working for *The Guardian Sport*. Caring about what people thought of my wrestling fandom had ended a long time previously; it kind of comes with the territory and it is a constant source of creative inspiration to me, so I embrace it. The wrestlers are storytellers and athletes and, contrary to the assumptions of every girl I have ever dated, I understand that they are not *actually* caving each other's heads in with a steel chair. I tell you this not to indulge myself, but to emphasize that my passions in day-to-day life are rich sources of valuable motivation. So are yours, whatever they may be.

Vince McMahon, the chairman of WWE, to me, is right up on that pedestal with Damon Albarn and he is the man responsible for pioneering pay-per-view televised sporting events as we know them today. He took professional wrestling from being a localized territory-based affair, with extremely limited TV programming time, to a global phenomenon with a showpiece event, Wrestlemania, as big as the Super Bowl or the football World Cup, and I was about to work for him.

The call to Dave's American mobile phone cost me £120, but we got along straight away and he liked my work – I'd have paid three times that amount and then some if it meant it could heighten my chances of attaining my dream client. Dave grew up in Bolton so, geographically, we had a personal connection. We talked Manchester, football, Bolton Wanderers and my own Leeds United. He promised me that he would do his best to find a way to use my work within the company, but warned I would have to be patient; it often took time to convince people to run with the more creative ideas in such a giant corporation like WWE. I assumed he was being nice to me, unable to terminate my dream with brutal honesty.

Mocking up increasing numbers of WWE samples, I showed no let up now that my hopes had been raised. Addicted to the fantasy, I said goodbye to moderation. He gave me generous, valuable feedback on the work I sent him, exhibiting the same honesty that Danny Allison had fired at me. He didn't have to share his industry experience like this, but he did and I embraced every word.

As I packed up to leave the office one day, the art director of *WWE Kids* magazine sent me an email, asking if I would be interested in illustrating a portrait of The Rock for the next issue. Had the chair not been directly behind me, I'd have fallen into the pillar behind my desk and onto the floor like one of those 1960s teenagers you see being carried by the police at Beatles gigs after passing out from sensory overload. Clearly, Dave had something to do with this.

I felt like I should be leaping around, smashing stuff up in unadulterated ecstasy. Maybe I should have dragged Rupert, the manager of the place I was currently working from, down to the floor and put him in the Kimora Lock submission hold. I'd watched Brock Lesnar do it enough times to feel confident enough that he would be tapping out in seconds. But I didn't do any of the above. I just slumped back in my seat with a silly, empty grin on my face and felt a wave of elation ride over me, now certain my refusal to quit during even the bleakest Monday mornings had been the right call.

Rupert walked past me to make tea for the office staff and I just looked right through him, not even aware I was staring. I was on cloud nine, imagining myself hoisting the Intercontinental Championship in the air as the audience came unglued. I wondered if WWE had ever commissioned an action figure for one of their production staff? I doubt it, but that didn't stop me imagining the silly scenario.

Rupert stood by my desk, asking if I was ok. He said I looked like I could do with a cup of coffee. I asked for a strong one and practically pinned him in the corner, telling him that I would be illustrating The Rock. Everybody knows Dwayne 'The Rock' Johnson, one of Vince McMahon's greatest creations. He won everything there was to win in WWE before heading to Hollywood to become one of their highest earners. Few people would truly understand how much this meant to me. I had landed my hand-picked, number one client in only three years of freelancing full-time. How had this happened? I don't suppose I'll ever truly process the euphoria that consumed me.

It turned out they had to get The Rock's personal approval of my illustration for image rights purposes, you see. I tell myself he stood there in full ring gear, trunks, boots and elbow pads, raising the people's eyebrow while a team of WWE magazine staff cowered.

WWE SET DESIGN

It didn't take long for a second commission to come through from Dave Hilton, designing a John Cena poster. Cena is this generation's Hulk Hogan, the champion and face of the WWE. Then he called me up on a rainy afternoon. Dave and I were in contact quite a lot by this point. We got along really well despite being separated by the Atlantic Ocean. We'd have this secret game of (despairing) text message tennis on the weekends when Leeds United or Bolton Wanderers crashed and burned again.

He called to ask about some painted banners he'd seen in my portfolio. For *The Lost Generation*, I had continued and developed the set design I had created for the Quenched Music photo shoot, painting lettering and naïve, simple images on lining paper banners, and now they featured in my online portfolio from that film. The WWE creative team was limited in its options for photo shoot locations and everything they did had to be carried out backstage at the arenas where the television show tapings took place. This meant that a lot of digital backgrounds had to be employed for major features and publication covers since boiler rooms and shutters only had so much mileage. My banners, Dave said, would give him something different to work with, something organic. He ended the conversation by saying he had to go for a meeting with Triple H and Stephanie.

On that bombshell I almost wet myself. Then as I lay back, supported by the ropes, dazed, he asked me to have a think about how realistic it would be to create 15 of the banners as set design to be hung up and lit behind the wrestling bad guys. Boom! The knockout blow had been landed, I was out for the count. I said I'd think it over, before putting the phone down and imploding.

My subconscious mind acted as a kind of safety net, retaining key words 'banner' and '15' but, in truth, I had been jabbed and left dizzy at the mention of 'Triple H' and 'Stephanie' (two of the biggest on-screen superstars of the past 15

215 |

years; WWE TV royalty) and this dream job query had hit me square on the chin. I was the freelance champion of south Manchester, the high wizard of my art kingdom. Having heard my guttural wail, when I returned to the room, Danni Skerritt was now stood behind where I slumped in my office chair, massaging my shoulders. Reviving me slowly.

Throughout the duration of the job, I played constant footage of WWE events over the years, fully indulging myself. I sporadically called anyone able to pick up the phone in working hours and told them about it. After a five-day lock-down in my living room, with ink-covered sheets hanging from every available surface, I took down and rolled up 15 complete and approved banners and couriered them to Stamford, Connecticut, USA. These were the set design for *WWE Magazine's 'Faces Of Evil'* feature and my career was essentially in those tubes, at the mercy of a string of delivery drivers and airport baggage-handlers. I watched the Fedex tracking service for a nerve-wracking 24 hours, refreshing the page a record number of times before the magical 'arrived' notification showed on my screen. Ultimate relief. I could get some sleep now. Dave text messaged me to say he had the banners in his hands and I needed a lie down to process everything that had just happened.

LISTEN UP AND LISTEN GOOD

Dave Hilton and I have been out for beers on several occasions and the guy is selfless, kind and down-to-earth. He was the creative director of *Maxim* Magazine in the US and has more than two decades of creative industries experience, working for publishing industry legend Felix Dennis, a man I sadly never got to meet, but has inspired me greatly nonetheless. I had served my purpose on the jobs Dave had given me, so had no reason to continue our conversation until we met for drinks in New York or in the UK. But he continued to stay in contact and drip-feed me tips and snippets of creative advice. Prior to the *Faces Of Evil* job, it had not once occurred to me that my artwork might transcend being used simply as the focal point of a job, such as a cover illustration of the centre of a piece of packaging. Here, photography was the driving force, yet in a three-dimensional environment, it couldn't have worked better, my artwork enhancing the image in a unique manner, playing the role of a set design. Dave's vast industry experience had enabled him to envision my art working in that way and now, something had been unlocked in the way I viewed the potential uses of my creations.

He started to send me links to interestingly presented work, asking me to think about how I could change the dynamic of my portfolio for the better. Then he asked me to create a double-page spread headline in my hand-painted lettering style. I struggled greatly for five days, almost missing a deadline for the first time, attempting to find a fluid brushstroke and consistent lettering style, which was incredibly hard. We got it over the line in the end, but he stuck with me. He said that if I become confident and developed my hand-painted lettering well enough, he felt I could make good money with it. Now a significant portion of my portfolio and commissioned work is painted lettering that sits alongside or over the top of good photography and I'm in the process of launching it as a specialist service with its own brand. You simply cannot buy such valuable advice and Dave was giving it to me for free. I've seen many fail because they believed they didn't need to continue learning...

One morning recently, clearing out my wardrobe, I came across the VHS covers that I would make myself, during my school days. They made me laugh as they were offensively bad, but the moment holding the copy of *WWE Magazine* featuring my banners next to the VHS sleeves was a special one and made me realize I should embrace the entire process, not just seeing the finished article. All too often, I allow the moment to pass, giving in to stress and preoccupation with the end result.

The crappy video sleeves and the published current work represented signposts along the way in my career path. What began with pencil drawings of Hulk Hogan as a infant, progressed to handmade video sleeve layouts, an early indication that the world of design was one in which I might find a calling. I had arrived at this moment, holding my dream commission in my hands. None of this would have come to pass had I not followed my own interests and passions so wholeheartedly. Now, everything seemed possible.

COLLABORATIONS

With a renewed passion for my work, I started to get stuck into the 12-hour days again. When things are going well, sleep is harder to come by. The noise in my head when it hit the pillow was reaching a level where the neighbours would soon be complaining. It seemed that the minute I tried to close my eyes, an angry swarm of exciting ideas would overcome my hopes of rest. When it was all going wrong, I found it hard to get up in the mornings. Most creative people I've met struggle to get eight hours of sleep in a week, let alone in a night.

Moving on from my WWE set design, with my dream client under my belt at such an early stage, I wanted to get my teeth into some meaty, longer-term projects. I always enjoy editorial illustration, but its time-sensitive nature means the illustrations are in and out of the door before you get to indulge in research or enjoy the working process. I craved something that would make me complete a sketchbook, maybe take me on a journey to somewhere new. Danni Skerritt was developing quickly, given his weekly lessons in Logic. He was now putting together some really cool, original music and he seemed to go to another place during those sessions as we worked in the same room.

Watching Skerritt slowly get to grips with Logic on his Macbook, it became apparent that it allows you to make music that, 20 years ago, would have required a whole studio with expensive, specialist kit. He was making the most of its capabilities. I watched him sat there, his head down for hours at a time, crafting challenging sounds; beats from Bollywood, West African trance and everything in between, all in our room above a pub in Salford. On one track he sampled an American painter talking about the divine intervention she claimed would happen during the crafting of her art. I couldn't tell you why these crazy audio fusions worked, but they did.

The sampling of the American artist resulted in his debut single *Whizzing Through Time and Space*, and I immediately loved his sound. I loved what I was seeing each day on the desk next to me in the Black Lion. Skerritt had found his thing and became addicted. There was only ever going to be one person steering his creative direction. I demanded that I take charge of any photo shoots, record sleeves and supporting artwork. I also wanted to steer his on stage look and character development.

The ideas and things I had learned from being around on the set of *The Lost Generation* gave me many ideas and the experience I needed to work effectively with Skerritt, no longer feeling restricted to simply illustration. Dave Hilton's help had strengthened my belief that I could successfully create a visual identity for a musician and here was my opportunity to back that up with actions.

He had founded the new genre, which he coined 'electro-dub.' He said that it was essentially electronica tinged with dub step, sprinkled with a dash of 'ghost-drone' and already people were eager to be a part of this intriguing new sound. What he had in abundance was ready access to organic music talent through our Quenched Music network, so he brought in carefully selected instrumentalists and vocals to forge something totally new.

Dirty Freud, he told me, was this entity from another dimension who would jump right in Danni Skerritt's body and the magic would happen. We spent whole evenings discussing Dirty Freud's purpose in our time and what ghost-drone meant. He told me that Freud was only here in the present day to save us with his music.

This stuff was borderline science fiction, but it was real to me and my imagination kicked into overdrive. I'd been dying to get my teeth into something like this ever since I saw what Damon Albarn and Jamie Hewlett collaborate to create Gorillaz. It had taken me 12 years since college to learn how it could be done and now here was the missing link. His output was picking up speed and reaching a frightening rate with ever-improving quality. Dirty Freud trusted my art direction implicitly and I had an unprecedented creative licence.

Thanks to me, Freud wore a customized, painted heavy-duty bright yellow Israeli standard-issue gas mask that had survived long, hostile journeys and atmosphere changes on planets Titan, Mars, Jupiter, Saturn and HD 189733b, where it rained blue glass (sideways, if anyone asked). He told me secret stories about his inter-stellar travels, fighting wars in the past and in the future and I sat there like a child imbibing a fairytale. I started going to the library and spent time reading books on astronomy and the Aztecs. You should have seen the face of the journalist from Salford Online who came down to the Black Lion to interview Dirty Freud. The guy wasn't ready for any of this. His mouth literally fell open when Freud told the guy his origins and that he had come to save us with his beats in response to the normally simple question: 'Where are you from, originally?'

Skerritt owned the Dirty Freud persona and it created not just a sound, but an aura of mystique around his music. If things went well enough between our creative partnership, I couldn't entirely rule out Damon instructing EMI records to get on the phone demanding collaboration with us. After living my WWE dream, no matter how silly the notion, it all seemed somehow possible.

I called Danny Allison, who was now back in the UK and we went to Mars to direct Dirty Freud's first photo shoot. We took a packed lunch... Freud said that the meal deals were rubbish up there.

KEN GARLAND, BRITISH GRAPHIC DESIGNER AND AUTHOR OF *'THE FIRST THINGS FIRST MANIFESTO'*

'We cannot be all things to all people and social consciences can be very heavy things to hang around one's neck. What we can do is find out what we can do as individuals. I support my own causes, for example Water Aid, does wonderful work and water is the thing that life is built on. A small contribution is still a contribution. I can't change the world but I can change some part of it. If enough people take care of little bits of it then we can make a difference. It's about acquiring skills, finding people who need those skills who can pay you for them. What you do with your surplus money is up to you.'

METHOD IN MADNESS

My pace of creative development had picked up some speed. Applying the skills fine-tuned through illustration to music, film and set design had taught me much about the benefits of escaping my comfort zone and now my problem became the danger of trying to function on too many fronts.

I wanted to do something noteworthy, not drift from one discipline to the next, being moderately good, but never a master of anything in particular. I reminded myself that provided image-making was at the core of everything, it could only be a good thing to continue expanding my market. If I wasn't writing about the art lifestyle, I was drawing. If I wasn't drawing for magazines, I was painting sets for an indie film. If the film wasn't shooting, I was on other planets, directing photo shoots for Dirty Freud. This is the way I always hoped it would be. Sport, art and music, my life pillars, were becoming major lynchpins in my career. For the first time, I felt like I had earned the right to think of myself as more than just an illustrator. I don't quite know what I am and I kind of like that.

WITH A LITTLE HELP FROM MY FRIENDS

All this new diversity in my projects was exhilarating and from having almost faded out only months earlier, I now had to slow myself down at times before I took on too much and burned out.

When I scrolled through my phone book, I started to notice that the diverse group of individuals in my world were, in fact, an extremely versatile gang of talented professionals. In the freelance world, everyone is always skint, so skill swaps and favours are valuable commodities. Manchester was a big village. If you turned down a back street, there was always someone you knew, outside a pub, smoking a cigarette, or at least someone you knew through a friend. London was a little more overwhelming, but I had a healthy stable of people in valuable places down there too, even if it did gobble up any money I had whenever I visited.

My supporting network had started with Rich Taylor and had grown over the seven years since graduating. Sam Price and I had become good friends in London and he always knew people worth sharing a beer with. He was about to go freelance, leaving *The Big Issue*. Sam is a good graphic designer and art director who knows his kerning from his baselines and was an ideal person to call when I was completely belly up, exposed as an image-maker in a world of margins and point sizes.

CAMPAIGN DIRECTOR

Quenched Music still had no long-term direction. Our writers were numbering more than ten by now and that gave Danni and I time to think about the direction in which we'd like to take the business, while they provided editorial content. We were happy enough using the project as a vehicle to reach places we couldn't as freelancers.

CALM is a charity and stands for The Campaign Against Living Miserably. It was co-founded by Manchester music legend Tony Wilson. Wilson became aware of the high rate of young males taking their own lives in the UK and wanted to do something about that sad statistic. A month or so later, I was down in London and called CALM on the off chance they would be able to sneak me in for five minutes to go and visit their offices.

I spent an hour or so drinking strong coffee with some of the staff. They told me all about the charity's work. CALM helps anyone, regardless of genre, but the ratio of suicide is three guys to every girl, so the marketing is targeted exclusively at men. Females, as a general rule, tend to talk about sensitive issues and are more open than guys. From what I gathered, men get caught up in the sticky web of pride, shame, perceived weakness and assorted negative connotations that are associated with openly admitting that things are not going well in life.

I sat there, horrified, with my coffee tilted at an angle that gave me a wet crotch. I didn't care. I left the office, shocked and invigorated by the conversation we had, feeling that, as a reasonably happy person who has always had the support of a large number of genuine friends and a loving family, I had to do something with my skills to help CALM, no matter how small my contribution.

My return journey from London Euston to Manchester Piccadilly was spent fervently scrawling notes in my latest A6 sketchbook, making tiny diagrams and odd charts to gain an overview of the skills I had in my network. I wondered if I had the time, the skills and the trust in the people around me to carry out a full charity campaign. Was this going too far? It would be a huge challenge, but perhaps one worth investigating. Besides, I think it's healthy to feel challenged, otherwise, how can you progress?

Straight away, Skerritt agreed to curate an album as Dirty Freud. We could hopefully sell it to raise money and awareness for CALM. All the bands and musicians we had befriended through Quenched Music were extremely keen to come on board.

Then I called up Danny Allison. Danny is always up for *it*, it doesn't matter what *it* is. Spending 14 hours-a-day locked in a room with someone gives you this intrinsic understanding, almost symbiotic at times, so asking was just a formal act of courtesy. I badly paraphrased the last two hours' thoughts, that were only partially formed in my head, but asked him if he'd be game for doing any photography that might be required. He loved the idea and was similarly taken aback by the grim statistics. Danny has had his own tough times over the years. He was in.

It was critical that I could convince Sam Price. Without him, I had no graphic designers I could trust sufficiently for the scope of the campaign I had in mind. Luckily for me, he had just gone freelance and the creativity of my idea got his creative juices flowing. It was a project we could carry out independently and really own.

All that was left now was a direction. I turned ideas over in my head and eventually found an angle I felt could work. One thing I have noticed throughout all of this is the eccentricity of most creative people, whether they are extroverted or introverted. I had a conversation with a guy who said he was intrigued with the connection between creativity and mental health and we both agreed there were numerous strong connections between the two. He wondered whether people who were different created art, or whether art created people who were different. We never reached a conclusion but it made me think and I still haven't fathomed it.

My work gets me out of bed. It gives me a feeling of belonging to something worthwhile in a life that, in my case, would otherwise be littered with norms. When I am angry, I can sketch and write. When I'm sad, I express it in ways other than tears or violence. Some people can't or don't know how to do that and haven't ever found that thing that they truly love, so I decided this campaign should take on a form that highlights the emotional benefits of the arts and shows how accessible they can be for everyone.

I called it Express, which became Xpress because an 'X' looks a lot better from a design perspective. Skerritt and I wanted to run the campaign through Quenched Music, release the album and feature a range of people who work in the creative industries, discussing what their involvement in the arts does for them.

DANNY ALLISON: PHOTOGRAPHER AND ILLUSTRATOR, *TIME* MAGAZINE, BUDWEISER, BBC, EMI RECORDS.

'It's 100% fact that getting into illustration and photography lifted me out of depression. I think creative minds are super fragile in many different ways. Not necessarily weak, just more susceptible to… society, politics, all these things you're bombarded with every day. They become easily befuddled and art rescued me. I ended up going to university after suffering bouts of anxiety and depression and my problems were progressively lifted as I embarked on this journey to becoming a creative professional.

I still suffer the anxieties, of course, but who doesn't to a certain extent? It's just that now, I know how to express my feelings through photography and my artwork. The glory is, if you have something on your mind that you find hard, or maybe don't want to talk about, you can go and draw it out. Maybe it's that you have a problem to do with religion, or sexism, anything at all, you make a poster instead of voicing it to someone who might not understand your opinions or viewpoints. Suddenly its out! I'll post it online, then maybe somebody comments, and before you know it, you've found someone with similar thoughts on the matter, in that particular community. There's a family feeling about the arts, your art.'

TAKING THE LEAD

The challenge of directing a full charity campaign felt daunting. So far, I had run my own business, but the entire company started and ended with me.

There was no shortage of creative professionals to interview and photograph so I started to reach out to illustrators, writers, designers, artists of all kinds. I wanted to look deeper than simply showcasing their work and find out what drove them, what empowered, enriched and enraged them, how all those emotions could be funnelled into a positive space. I wanted to create a study of how artistic expression could give you space to put all those emotions in perspective.

Sam Price created the logo and a brand for the website which was simple with a layout that let the work speak for itself. It felt strange to have Sam sending me work that I was required to critique and approve, a role reversal after years of the opposite. If I was going to call myself 'director,' I couldn't shy away from the responsibility that came with such a title.

The main problem in a campaign to raise awareness was that I had no real access to anyone remotely famous, who might give the campaign some exposure beyond our limited existing audience. The currency of fame didn't hold any weight with me or the ethos of Xpress, but I figured that if we could attract the support and endorsement of someone who was recognizable, gained the respect of their peers for their artistic merit and whose profile transcended the art world, we would immediately make the campaign worthy of national press, maybe even give it global value. One or two PR companies showed a fleeting interest, but I felt that, with a recognized name or two, we could garner more support from those who could spread this further than us.

Thumping inanimate objects became a routine every time I called a celebrity agent who told me, 'no fee, no involvement from their client'. It became obvious, quite quickly, that without a budget of any description or a personal connection, we wouldn't be bringing in the red carpet royalty and I found it frustrating. But when you consider the number of these requests celebrities must receive every day, it adds up. Daniel Radcliffe's PA came very close to allowing me to interview him, but in the end, his schedule was so full that they had to decline. She told me they get around 15 requests a day from such charitable organisations.

I started to look a little closer to home. Jon McClure, frontman of Reverend and the Makers was using Twitter to great effect to promote his band and I wondered if our chance encounter at Unconvention my help me reach him.

Jon surprisingly remembered our interview and gave me his phone number. Suicide had taken the lives of several of his family members. The cause was one close to his heart. He agreed to give us an interview and be photographed. He also granted us the use of a Reverend and the Makers track for the Xpress album.

Ian Stone, a comedian who was writing a column for the monthly *Arsenal magazine*, was aware of my illustration work for the club. The editor put me in touch with Ian, and he followed Jon's lead. I came to London to talk to him about his work in comedy and the benefits it brought him. Danny Dyer, Caitlin Rose and UK slam poetry champion Mark Mace Smith followed a nice selection of lesser-known creative people who agreed to support our campaign.

We began to earn some nice plaudits. Danny Dyer is an East London actor who has been typecast as a cockney hard man, but we found him to be a gentleman who revealed his human side in our interview, one his manager said was among the best he had ever given. His involvement gave us a real boost and helped project the campaign beyond local confines.

I somehow pulled out an ace by bringing on board Ricky Gervais' long-term collaborator, writer, actor and comedian, Stephen Merchant. The podcasts those guys did with Karl Pilkington had seen me through my homesickness in New Zealand, so I couldn't have been happier and Stephen provided us with a really big name with which to champion CALM's work.

Browsing the creative press one afternoon in Magma, a creative bookstore with outlets in London and Manchester, I saw an *Eye* Magazine article on Ken Garland. Ever since studying Ken's career for my dissertation, I had esteemed the guy in godlike admiration and had only rarely returned to see what he was up to. Having seen this, I emailed him to ask about the possibility of interviewing him for Xpress. He invited me to London and I spent a wonderful hour in his studio, divided only by a coffee table and 50 years' experience. We talked graphic activism, travelling the world and our mutual connection to Central Saint Martins College and he gave me a free copy of his own retrospective book!

Each of these people brought another original angle to the campaign and we set about working on the charity album. We raised just under £1,000 through crowdfunding, which wasn't a lot, but enough for us to produce 1,000 physical copies of the album with the addition of sponsorship by my illustration agency and a local startup mobile phone company. The Strokes and The Libertines signed up alongside Reverend and the Makers so bring some serious heavyweight names to the album to complement the new bands we had included.

Working in music had taught me just how hard it is for new musicians these days. The fast pace of technology means it is now easier to steal music and film than it is pay for it. So far more emphasis has to be placed on live music revenue and licensing opportunities. Many brands now sponsor events, albums and so on, and advertisements on TV, radio and online are good sources of income for bands who can find the publishers who will assist them in finding the right commercial use for their music.

What I hadn't bargained for during the Xpress charity campaign was a crash course in the legalities of licensing music. The PRS is the UK's main royalty collection service. So musicians sign up with it for a fee, register tracks and if the tracks are ever used, *anywhere,* the PRS bills them on behalf of the artist. It's why you're not allowed to air music to the public outside your home without a PRS licence. For our physical copies, we had to go through the licensing process. My brain turned to mush and, given that I was already very busy with illustration work, I found myself on the verge of tears during all of this. As an illustrator who had recently had his confidence smashed to pieces while looking at the job listings, for which I was utterly unqualified, this roughhouse apprenticeship in just about everything restored my belief in my ability to adapt. You come out of these tough spells feeling stronger than before, a rough graduation that makes progression ultimately more satisfying than before.

Xpress was a storm of worthwhile stress and creative learning curves, consolidating the journey I had been on to this point, in one beast of a project. Australian rapper Tuka said the most beautiful thing during his interview and it really summed up what we were trying to do, in a sense: 'What a person is truly good at comes so naturally to them that often they do not even see it as a talent, overlooking the thing they're truly good at.'

When I started Xpress, I said that if just one person said to us that they had taken something positive from our work and helped themselves, then the campaign would be a success. We had quite a few people approach us in various ways and tell us they felt they could now talk openly about their problems thanks to the less daunting context in which our campaign had placed real issues. Some of those were close friends, who I had no idea were dealing with any issues.

TEA WITH HEROES

Entering my sixth year as a freelancer, I'm starting a new chapter in London. Danni Skerritt is bound for fatherhood for the first time, whilst aspiring to musical greatness, so it was the right time for us both to leave the madhouse.

I'm back down to zero regular clients, but I've grown accustomed to riding the madness of this freelance world and through all these galvanizing experiences, I have confidence in my ability as an artist and feel I can adapt to changes both positive and negative. The work is still regular, just more unpredictable with the occasional dry spell. After a while, you learn not to panic or get too excited when things are up and down, just to go with it and keep the faith. It's simply the nature of the beast and I suppose it always will be.

It's exciting to be in a city where any chance encounter can lead to new places and experiences and also a little terrifying given the inflated living costs, but it's all a big game of risk. Last time I lost most of my clients, I hid in my bedroom and wrote angry blogs. This time, I bought a London travel card for one year upfront, I have my camera, Macbook and I signed up for my own studio, by the River Thames at Second Floor Studios and Arts, a project that houses more than 400 creative professionals in a former industrial unit. I plan to be a bigger nuisance than ever before and in a city with this many people, I'll never run out of ears to chew.

I'm at another crossroads, with all these options ahead of me, but if I didn't arrive at them on a regular basis, I'd be concerned. The fact that these decisions are even there to make is a huge sign of progression. Do I pursue a career in film art direction, continue to develop my illustration style and take it new places, write some more or push Quenched Music? Probably a fusion of all of the above and whatever feels right at any given time. I think the variation in projects allows me to keep each one fresh.

There's always the stress, always the guilt and usually the money comes and goes. But this year, I got to go to Wrestlemania 30 in New Orleans and the WWE Hall Of Fame ceremony thanks to my work with the company. I was shown around the HQ offices where I saw the sketches and mockups of my work on the walls of Dave Hilton's office and I felt like a teenager again.

For all the challenges a life in the arts throws at you on a daily basis, I wouldn't change it for anything, it's what makes it so attractive and repulsive when you don't know what is coming on any given day. How else would I drink tea with my heroes, live out childhood dreams and work while travelling around on the other side of the world?

ABOUT THE AUTHOR

Ben Tallon is an internationally established illustrator and creative director of Quenched Music.

His vibrant illustration, hand painted lettering and unique set design in film and television has become an integral part of such pop-culture brands as E4's *Skins*, *The Guardian*, World Wrestling Entertainment, Arsenal Football Club and *Mixmag* among many others.

Growing up in late 1980s and early 1990s West Yorkshire, Ben's love of drawing his heroes, from Leeds United Football Club, World Wrestling Entertainment, Damon Albarn and video games led him to pursue a creative education and a career in the arts.

He now lives in London but continues to suffer at the hands of his dysfunctional football team.

Champagne and Wax Crayons; Riding the Madness of the Creative Industries is Ben's first book.

www.bentallon.com

SPEAKER INFORMATION

BEN TALLON is an expert speaker on topics including:

- Starting and surviving in the arts
- Freelance creative lifestyle
- Originality in the illustration market
- Branching out into other creative fields
- People and self-promotion